ABC's of Type

ABC's of Type

ALLAN HALEY

WATSON-GUPTILL PUBLICATIONS/NEW YORK
A STEP-BY-STEP PUBLISHING BOOK

For Lang and Toby

I am deeply indebted to many people, without whose support and help this book would not have been possible. First there is my family, who let me hide out on Saturday and Sunday mornings (my favorite time to write). Then there is Nancy Aldrich-Ruenzel and Catharine Fishel at *Step-By-Step Graphics,* who made possible the original articles that became the chapters of this book. Next is Karen Nagle, who typed my manuscript with patience and skill. Acknowledgment is also due to Sid Timm, who edited my work and made it better—much better.

Typeface headings, alphabets, and family listings appear courtesy of Linotype Company. The typeface names Helvetica, Memphis, Optima, Palatino, Times Roman, and Univers are trademarks of Linotype AG and/or its Subsidiaries. ITC Avant Garde Gothic, ITC Cheltenham, ITC Galliard, ITC Garamond, ITC Korinna, and ITC Souvenir are trademarks of the International Typeface Corporation. Gill Sans is a trademark of the Monotype Corporation.

Copyright © Step-By-Step Publishing and Allan Haley

First published in 1990 in New York by Watson-Guptill Publications, a division of BPI Communications, Inc., 1515 Broadway, New York, N.Y. 10036

Library of Congress Cataloging-in-Publication Data

Haley, Allan.
    The ABC's of type : a guide to contemporary typefaces / Allan Haley.
       p.   cm.
    "A Step-by-step publishing book."
    Includes bibliographical references.
    ISBN 0–8230–0053–2
    1. Printing—Specimens. 2. Type and type-founding. I. Title.
Z250.H2 1990
686.2'24—dc20   89–21495
                               CIP

Published in the United Kingdom by
Lund Humphries Limited,
16 Pembridge Road, London W11.
ISBN 0-85331-580-9

A CIP catalogue record for this book is available from the British Library.

Manufactured in the United States of America

First printing, 1990

1 2 3 4 5 6 7 8 9 10 / 95 94 93 92 91 90

CONTENTS

Introduction

When I was young, I wanted to be an artist. I took art classes as early as kindergarten, but it wasn't until high school that I was permitted to enroll in a life-drawing class. Two weeks into that class, the art instructor was making her normal rounds, looking at each student's work. When she got to my drawing, she paused for a moment and then asked me a question: "What do you like? What interests you?"

"Girls!" was my immediate answer.

"Besides girls," she said.

This time my answer was slower in coming: "Football, surfing, cars, I guess."

"Good!" she said. "Draw cars, and study anatomy."

Her point was that something cannot be drawn properly without being understood. I understood cars, I knew how they worked. I didn't understand anatomy (or girls, for that matter), and as a result, my renderings were less successful than they could have been.

I studied anatomy; and found that my instructor was right. The more I learned, the better my life drawings became.

And so it is with typography. The more you know about typefaces, the better you are able to use them. Using typefaces to communicate graphic messages is what typography is all about.

The point of this book is to provide practical information about typefaces, with each chapter dedicated to a particular typestyle. Chapters are divided into three parts: "Attributes," "Background," and "Considerations for Use." Thus *The ABC's of Type*.

There are those who would have you believe that identifying the attributes of any particular typeface is a waste of time. These folks argue that typeface attributes are, for the most part, obvious, and that all one has to do is look at a typeface to be able to determine its attributes. The problem is that most of us tend to look at things (especially things typographic) without really seeing them. We can readily distinguish Times Roman from Optima; but Rockwell from Memphis becomes a little more difficult, and Helvetica from Univers (at times) is a downright struggle.

The reason for the "Attributes" portion of *The ABC's of Type* is to differentiate various typeface designs. Not only do you get to know the various typographic tools a little better, you also acquire the edge of being able to use them better. Univers and Helvetica, for example, may look very similar, but if you know the attributes of the two designs you will know that Univers is the more carefully

thought-out and structured type family. It benefits from slightly more contrast in stroke thickness; you might want to choose it over Helvetica to solve a design problem that calls for high degrees of readability in a document requiring multiple typeface changes.

In addition, it is fun to have a little insight into the history and design characteristics of the typefaces you use, hence the "Background" discussions. Knowing the "Attributes" of a typeface will help you spot it in a crowd and perhaps match it to a particular application. Understanding the "Background" of a typestyle will enable you to fix it in time and in the typographic spectrum. All of this is nice, but not terribly practical information—unless you want to know how to use the type best to solve real-world graphic problems.

The "Considerations for Use" section of each chapter is aimed at providing some practical guidelines for typeface usage. It will cover areas like: mixing of typestyles, handling white space, size considerations, font availability, letter-spacing, and word spacing. Although no two sections are exactly the same, the goal of each is consistent: to help the graphic communicator get the most out of the type design.

TYPE FAMILIES

A lot of typographic benefits, which many of us grew up with and take for granted, were not available to designers even one generation ago. We have come to expect our type suppliers to provide automatic kerning, but until the 1970s, this was a process limited to the most exclusive (and expensive) typographic communication. Small caps, hanging figures, and an array of ligatured characters were only available in a few typestyles—and then only from the best-equipped typographers. Complicated run-arounds were virtually impossible. Simple tight letterspacing was impossible.

Type used to be made out of lead, a very tangible, but relatively inflexible, medium. Today, type is electronic data—something that cannot be held (or even seen until it is imaged on film or paper) but is wonderfully flexible. Where only a few decades ago type placement and arrangement were held within the confines of rigid little blocks of metal, now typography is only limited by the designer's imagination.

The idea of type families, however, has been around for a long time. As early as 1488, Moritz Brandis of Leipzig created a semibold font to complement a basic text face. Although families have been part of typographic tradition for a long time, they didn't become popular until the American Type Founders Company (ATF) was formed in the 1890s. This large and exceptionally influential organization was formed through a merger of more than twenty independent typefounders scattered across the United States. Each company had its own type library of hundreds of typestyles, many of which duplicated styles offered by other companies. The task of organizing this massive typographic resource became the responsibility of Morris Fuller Benton. In an attempt to bring some standardization to the ATF type offering, he grouped all the designs with similar traits under a generic name. Thus, Old Style Antique and Catalogue Antique, two faces of virtually the same design from two separate manufacturers, both became Bookman, and Thorne Fat

Face and Poster Roman No. 3 eventually became parts of the Bodoni family because of their many similarities with this typestyle.

In addition to organizing their existing resources, ATF began to release new typestyles within family groupings. A few families were complete at the time of release, and others continued to grow as a response to customer demand. The Cheltenham family, for example, grew from the two faces of the original release in 1904 to a family of more than twenty faces eight years later. Since the advent of phototype technology in the early 1970s, complete type families can be planned and designed before any faces are actually produced.

A type family consists of a number of typefaces that show a marked resemblance but have individual design variances, such as weight, proportion, angle, surface texture, and, in some cases, even design. Although the members of a typeface family may be varied and diverse, all maintain the basic characteristics of the parent design—in much the same way that brothers and sisters look like their parents.

Weight. The most common and obvious variation within a type family is weight. Typestyles can have very light to extremely heavy stroke widths and still maintain family design traits. There is a British standard that classifies stroke

weight changes in eight graduations: extra light, light, semilight, medium (usually the basic weight of the family), semibold, bold, extra bold, and ultra bold. Two other common weights not covered under the British standard are book, a midpoint between light and medium, and black, which is usually considered bolder than ultra bold. There are also many other names, such as fat, slim, hairline, elephant, and massive, to describe type family weight changes. There are even some families (Univers was one of the first) that use a numerical code to, among other things, distinguish typeface weights.

Proportion. Character proportion is another variation on a family theme. By various stages, typestyles can be condensed or proportionally expanded from the parent design. Standard proportional increments are known as ultra condensed, extra condensed, condensed, normal, expanded, extra expanded, and ultra expanded. Other terms are also common, especially with display typestyles. Condensed proportions are sometimes referred to as compressed, elongated, or narrow, and expanded designs in some type families are classified as wide, extended, or stretched. In most typeface families, however, the degree of proportion changes are limited, and condensed designs are more prevalent than expanded ones.

Latin Bold Condensed

Latin Bold

Latin Wide

Type family proportions.

Obliqued

Slanted roman design.

Cursive

Italic based on classic handwriting.

OUTLINE

THREE DIMENSIONAL

Incised

STENCIL

TEXTURE

Comstock

Reverse

Family textures.

Angle. The design that results from changing the angle of a typestyle is called italic. This variation includes both simple oblique letters and a true cursive design. Originally, italic letters were created as an independent design, based on formalized handwriting. Many years passed before the italic typeface was included as part of the type family, and many more before it was actually designed as a complement to the roman face.

Italics based on classical handwriting are generally called cursives and have an almost script-like quality to them. Cursive designs are almost exclusively confined to serif typestyles. Obliques appear to be just slanted letters and are usually the italic designs of sans serif typefaces.

Surface Texture. Surface texture is another variant within a type family. There are outline designs, typestyles that have the appearance of three-dimensionally incised, stenciled, textured, and comstocked typefaces.

Design. There are even typeface families that are made up of different subfamilies. ITC Stone is a perfect example. The subgroups consist of Serif, Sans, and something called Informal. Each design has roman and italic versions in three weights for a total of eighteen individual typefaces. The three basic designs have the same cap heights, lowercase x-heights, stem weights, and general proportions. Each typeface has been designed to stand on its own as a useful communications tool but is also part of a large integrated family that can be mixed easily with other members of the family.

Type families, like families of people, provide continuity, consistency, and a built-in support group.

Stone Serif Medium

Stone Serif Medium Italic

Stone Serif Semi Bold

Stone Serif Semi Bold Italic

Stone Serif Bold

Stone Serif Bold Italic

Stone Sans Serif Medium

Stone Sans Serif Medium Italic

Stone Sans Serif Semi Bold

Stone Sans Serif Semi Bold Italic

Stone Sans Serif Bold

Stone Sans Serif Bold Italic

The ITC Stone family consists of subgroups, including serif and sans serif styles. Each design has roman and italic versions in three weights.

A Practical Guide to Type Classification

There are over three thousand typefaces readily available to the graphic designer; with a little searching at least a thousand or so more can also be included in a typographic "tool box." That's a lot!

In an attempt to provide some order to this menagerie, a guide to type classification has been included in this book. It isn't definitive, but it should prove to be a valuable reference tool.

Working with type is, for the most part, pretty straightforward stuff. If you don't know the "rule" for a particular circumstance, common sense will almost always provide the correct answer. But there are exceptions. Take, for example, typeface classifications: Bodoni, often labeled as the "quintessential Modern" type, was created over two hundred years ago, whereas ITC Weidemann, released just a few years ago, is referred to as an "Old Style" type. Type can be a nebulous animal. A typeface's name may give no clue as to its family or origin—indeed, it may even be misleading. In addition, the cosmos of faces available today may appear to be similar in outward characteristics, but each is actually quite different.

Common sense may not always reign supreme when it comes to typeface classification, yet the process of categorizing type provides a number of benefits. It can help facilitate the identification of a particular typeface, aid in the selection of suitable substitutions when the typeface of first choice is not available, and determine the best style of type for a particular application. Good typeface classification systems can also provide some continuity to what would otherwise be a confusing array of typeface designs. It makes sense to have logical type groupings. But where to start?

The most basic system divides typefaces into two categories: those with serifs and those without. This is a good start but certainly not very practical for any real work. As a result, many typographic scholars have taken this basic foundation and built more elaborate systems over the years—some with over a hundred different categories.

Two categories of type are inadequate for any meaningful work, but hundreds can become self-defeating. A compromise between the two extremes utilizes nine basic groups, some of which are further subdivided for added clarity.

There may be some differences between this and other systems (there may even be some disagreements concerning the placement of a typeface or two), but its intent is to provide a working *guideline* for the typographic communicator—with emphasis on the word *guideline*.

The good news is that few things typographical can be confined to "either/or" regulation. So even if this group of categories is not perfect, neither is it wrong.

OLD STYLE

These are the first roman types, which were created or designed between the late-fifteenth and mid-eighteenth centuries. In Old Style types, the axis of curved strokes is normally inclined to the left, so that weight stress is at approximately eight and two o'clock. The contrast in stroke weight is not dramatic, and hairlines tend to be on the heavy side. Serifs are almost always bracketed in Old Style designs and head serifs (the ones at the top of letters) are often angled.

Venetian Old Style. These are the first Old Style faces, created in Venice around 1470. Generally, they take their style and proportions from handwritten letters drawn with an obliquely held broad pen. A dead giveaway for Venetian Old Style designs is the diagonal cross stroke of the lowercase *e*; almost every example has one. Venetian Old Styles also have only minor contrast in character-stroke thickness, and serifs are heavily bracketed.

Aldine Old Style. Aldine Old Style designs are based on the original work of Aldus Manutius in the early 1490s. During the sixteenth century the Aldine model was adopted and followed first in France, then in the rest of Europe. (It is probably one of the first typefaces to have been copied widely—sort of the Helvetica of its day.) Aldine Old Style typefaces generally have more contrast in stroke weight than Venetian Old Style designs, and the lowercase *e* crossbar is almost always horizontal. Serif bracketing is also obvious but usually not as pronounced as in earlier designs.

Dutch Old Style. In the Netherlands, the larger x-height, darker color, and greater contrast in stroke weight of the German black letter were melded with Aldine design traits, resulting in Dutch Old Style designs. This style of type first appeared in the mid-sixteenth century but continued to be developed and refined into the twentieth century. Dutch Old Styles are heavy types that tend to be exceptionally legible and highly readable even under the most hostile conditions.

Old Style/Revivals. There are two "catch-all" categories in this identification system. One category is Old Style/Revival, which can display a predominance of Old Style design traits but is generally not patterned after any particular type of the period. Often, in fact, Old Style/Revivals share several design influences. As with other Old Style designs, however, character stroke is relatively conservative, weight stress is inclined, and serifs are bracketed.

By definition, these are types developed after the original Old Styles, and many currently popular designs fit into this category; therefore, the list of typical designs shown in the chart has been expanded to include recent faces.

TRANSITIONAL

The style for these typefaces was established in the mid-eighteenth century, primarily by the English printer and ty-

CG Cloister

ABCDEFGHIJKLMNOPQRSTUVWXYZ&
abcdefghijklmnopqrstuvwxyz1234567890
(.,:;''*?¿!¡)%¢$/£ÇÑçéíñß

ff ffi fi ffl fl

TASTE IN PRINTING DETERMINES THE FORM TYPOGRAPHY IS TO
take. The selection of a congruous typeface, the quality and suitability for its purpose of
the paper to be used, the care and labor, time and cost of materials devoted to its produc

ITC Usherwood Medium

ABCDEFGHIJKLMNOPQRSTUVWXYZ&
abcdefghijklmnopqrstuvwxyz1234567890
(.,:;''*?¿!¡)%¢$/£ÇÑçéíñß

ABCDEFGHIJKLMNOPQRSTUVWXYZ&
ff ffi fi ffl fl1234567890

TASTE IN PRINTING DETERMINES WHAT FORM TYPOGRAPHY SHALL
TAKE. THE SELECTION OF A CONGRUOUS TYPEFACE, THE QUALITY AND SUI
tability for its purpose of the paper to be used, the care and labor, time

ITC Fenice Regular

ABCDEFGHIJKLMNOPQRSTUVWXYZ&
abcdefghijklmnopqrstuvwxyz1234567890
(.,:;''*?¿!¡)% ¢$/ÇÑçéíñß

Typography is the selection of a

Bookman
14 point
ABCDEFGHIJKLMNOPQRSTUVWXYZ&
abcdefghijklmnopqrstuvwxyz1234567890
(.,:;''*?¿!¡)%¢$/ÇÑçéíñß
Unique Complement Characters
ACGK MNR S℔&fhkmnofrstvwy
24 point
Typography is the selection of

Examples of four typestyles with serifs (top to bottom): Venetian Old Style (Cloister);
Transitional (Usherwood); Twentieth-Century Modern (Fenice); and Nineteenth-Century
Clarendon (Bookman). From *The Type Book*, by the Compugraphic Corporation.

pographer John Baskerville. His ground-breaking work with calendared paper and printing methods allowed very fine character strokes to be reproduced and subtle character shapes to be maintained. The axis of curve strokes can be inclined in transitional typefaces, but it generally has a vertical stress. Weight contrast is more pronounced than in Old Style designs. Serifs are still bracketed and head serifs are oblique. These typefaces represent the transition between Old Style and Modern designs and incorporate characteristics of each. (Recent designs are included in the chart on page 17.)

MODERN

The work of Giambattista Bodoni in the eighteenth century epitomizes the Modern style of type. Moderns, when first released, were called "Classical" designs. It soon became apparent, however, that they were not updated versions of classic typestyles but altogether new designs. Here, contrast between thick and thin strokes is abrupt and dramatic. The axis of curved strokes is vertical, with little or no bracketing. These tend to be highly mannered designs that are obviously constructed rather than drawn. Moderns are plagued by the dreaded typographic disease of dazzling. Their strong vertical stress creates a "picket fence" appearance, which tends to vibrate on the page. These are the aristocrats of type: beautiful to look at, but they should be approached with caution.

Didone Modern. These are typefaces created during the eighteenth century or the direct descendants of those typefaces. They set the standard for Modern types. Some designs have slight, almost imperceptible, serif bracketing; however, most have none, and serifs are generally not much more than simple hairlines stuck onto the ends of vertical strokes. Didones normally have slightly heavier hairline strokes than twentieth-century Moderns.

In many cases, stroke terminals are ball shapes rather than the reflection of a broad pen.

Twentieth-Century Modern. These typefaces were created in the twentieth century, and although they may share many design traits with Didones, they generally are not intended to be revivals of those earlier designs. Twentieth-century Moderns also tend to be more stylized than their predecessors.

CLARENDON

This style of type first became popular in the 1850s. Like the Didones before them, Clarendons have a strong vertical weight stress, but this is where the similarities end. They can have obvious contrast in stroke thickness, but it is not nearly as dramatic as in the Didones. In addition, serifs are normally heavy, bracketed, and usually square-cut. These are the typographic workhorses: robust designs that can tackle virtually any task with predictably successful results. They may not be especially attractive or sophisticated, but they get the job done.

Nineteenth-Century Clarendon. As the name implies, these are the first-released Clarendon typestyles. Their stroke-weight contrast is least pronounced, and their serifs tend to be short to medium in length. Many of these designs were initially released as display types, and relatively few made the transition from foundry to machine-set type.

Neo Clarendon. These typefaces are twentieth-century versions of the first Clarendon designs. Contrast in character stroke weight is more obvious, and serifs tend to be longer than in earlier designs. Some versions also share design traits with other categories. Twentieth-century Clarendons are the natural product of evolution from the first display versions. They are generally more sophisticated and perform exceptionally well as text.

Legibility/Clarendon. This style of type was first released in the 1920s and is the final link in the Clarendon evolutionary chain. Contrast in stroke weight is kept to a minimum, serifs tend to be on the short side, and x-heights are usually large. These typefaces were specifically designed to be highly legible and easy to read in a variety of typographic environments. They may not be striking in design, but they are the hardest workers of the Clarendon group.

SLAB SERIF

These typefaces have very heavy serifs with no, or exceptionally slight, bracketing. Generally, changes in stroke weight are imperceptible. Too many slab serif typestyles appear to be sans serif designs with the simple addition of heavy (stroke-weight) serifs. Slab serifs are exceptionally durable and tend to evoke a feeling of straightforward reliability in text composition. They are also versatile display designs.

GLYPHIC

Typefaces in this category tend to reflect lapidary inscriptions rather than pen-drawn text. Contrast in their stroke weight is usually at a minimum, and the axis of curved strokes tends to be vertical. The distinguishing feature of the glyphic typefaces is the triangular-shaped serif design; in some faces, this is modified to a flaring of the character strokes where they terminate. In some classification systems, this one category is broken up into two groups: glyphic and Latin. Latins are the faces with strictly triangular-shaped serifs.

SANS SERIF

These are typefaces without serifs (*sans,* from the French, meaning "without"). Although stone-cut versions of the style predate printing with movable type, the first typographic use of sans serif letters was in 1816 by William Caslon IV (a descendant of William Caslon, who designed the important serif typestyle bearing his name). Aside from their lack of serifs, the most distinctive quality of sans serif typefaces is their tendency toward an optically monotone stroke weight, which some typophiles feel hinders the type's effectiveness in text composition—even more so than their lack of serifs. Early sans serif types were called Grotesques because they were generally regarded as being ugly. In England, they are still called Grotesques.

Grotesque Sans Serif. These are the first commercially popular sans serif typefaces. Contrast in stroke weight is most apparent in these styles; there is a slightly "squared" quality to many of the curves, and several designs have the "bowl and loop" lowercase *g* common to roman types. These are the personality types of the sans serif series—some even have a kind of homespun quality. In some cases, the *R* has a curled leg, and the *G* usually has a spur.

Neo Grotesque Sans Serif. These are sans serif designs patterned after the first Grotesques but more refined in form. Stroke contrast is less pronounced than in earlier designs, and much of the "squareness" in curved strokes is also lost. Neo Grotesques can easily be confused with their earlier counterparts. Normally the most obvious distinguishing characteristic of these faces is their single bowl *g*, more monotone weight stress, and lack of individual personality.

Geometric Sans Serif. Simple geometric shapes heavily influence the construction of these typefaces. Strokes have the appearance of being strict monolines, and character shapes are made up of seemingly perfect geometric forms. Geometric sans serif faces tend to be less readable than Grotesques.

Slab Serif
ITC Lubalin Graph Medium

ABCDEFGHIJKLMNOPQRSTUVWXYZ&
abcdefghijklmnopqrstuvwxyz1234567890

Glyphic
ITC Barcelona™ Book

ABCDEFGHIJKLMNOPQRSTUVWXYZ&
abcdefghijklmnopqrstuvwxyz1234567890

Sans Serif—Grotesque
News Gothic Bold

ABCDEFGHIJKLMNOPQRSTUVWXYZ&
abcdefghijklmnopqrstuvwxyz1234567890

Sans Serif—Neo Grotesque
ITC Franklin Gothic Medium

ABCDEFGHIJKLMNOPQRSTUVWXYZ&
abcdefghijklmnopqrstuvwxyz1234567890

Sans Serif—Geometric
ITC Kabel Medium

ABCDEFGHIJKLMNOPQRSTUVWXYZ&
abcdefghijklmnopqrstuvwxyz1234567890

Sans Serif—Humanistic
Goudy Sans Medium

ABCDEFGHIJKLMNOPQRSTUVWXYZ&
abcdefghijklmnopqrstuvwxyz1234567890

Sans Serif—Square
Antique Olive

ABCDEFGHIJKLMNOPQRSTUVWXYZ&
abcdefghijklmnopqrstuvwxyz1234567890

Scripts
Coronet Bold

ABCDEFGHIJKLMNOPQRSTUVWXYZ&
abcdefghijklmnopqrstuvwxyz1234567890

Graphic
Revue Regular

ABCDEFGHIJKLMNOPQRSTUVWXYZ&
abcdefghijklmnopqrstuvwxyz1234567890

Nine type styles generally categorized as sans serifs. From *The Type Book,* by the Compugraphic Corporation.

Humanistic Sans Serif. These are sans serif designs based on the proportions of roman inscriptional capitals and lowercase letters. In many cases, contrast in stroke weight is also readily apparent. Many claim that these are the most legible and most easily read of the sans serif types. They also most closely match roman design characteristics and proportions. Many also display a strong calligraphic influence.

Square Sans Serif. These designs are generally based on Grotesque or Neo Grotesque character traits and proportions, but they have a definite (and at times dramatic) squaring of normally curved strokes. They usually employ more latitude in character spacing than their more conventional sans serif cousins, and they tend to be exceptional display designs.

SCRIPTS

This category includes typefaces that imitate cursive writing. Script typefaces come in all shapes and sizes. Some are very elegant and appear to be carefully drawn with a quill pen, and others are the essence of spontaneity. In the interest of expediency and efficiency, all scripts are grouped here under one category. To do justice to these styles over a dozen different subcategories would have to be described, and since scripts are not used that much anyway, it is not necessary to give them undue exposure.

GRAPHIC

These typefaces defy pigeonholing. They can look like letters cut in stencil, imaged on a computer terminal, or decorated with flowers. Their only shared trait is that they have been constructed rather than "written" (the other catch-all category). Some are excellent communicators, others are not. In fact, some pretty thin excuses for type design fall into this category. (None of those, however, are represented here.)

CLASSIFICATION	TYPICAL DESIGNS
OLD STYLE	
Venetian	Bauer Text (or Schneidler Old Style), Centaur, Cloister, Deepdene, Kennerly, Italian Old Style
Aldine	Bembo, Cooper Old Style, Electra, Garamond, Goudy Old Style, Granjon, Palatino, Sabon, Weiss Roman
Dutch	Caslon, Concorde, Janson, Plantin, Times Roman
Revival	Belwe, ITC Benguiat, ITC Berkeley Old Style, Bramley, Breughel, ITC Caslon No. 224, ITC Clearface, Cooper Black, Edwardian, ITC Esprit, ITC Galliard, ITC Garamond, Italia, Lutetia, Magna Carta, Poppl-Pontifex, Worcester Round, ITC Souvenir, Trump Mediaeval, ITC Weidemann, Windsor
TRANSITIONAL	Americana, Baskerville, Bulmer, Caledonia, Concorde Nova, Fairfield, Garth Graphic, Leamington, ITC New Baskerville, Orion, Perpetua, ITC Usherwood, ITC Zapf International
MODERN	
Didone	Bauer Bodoni, Bodoni, Didot, Torino
Twentieth Century	Auriga, Centennial, Else, ITC Fenice, ITC Jamille, Linotype Modern, ITC Modern No. 216, Photina, Walbaum Book, ITC Zapf Book
CLARENDON	
Nineteenth Century	Bookman, Cheltenham, Cush Antique
Neo	ITC Bookman, ITC Century, Century Schoolbook, ITC Cheltenham, ITC Clearface, ITC Cushing, Fortune, Itek Bookface, ITC Korinna, Melior
Legibility	Clarion, Corona, Excelsior, Ionic No. 5, Modern, Nimrod, Olympian
SLAB SERIF	Aachen, Calvert, Cairo, City Egyptienne, Karnak, ITC Lubalin Graph, Memphis, Rockwell, Serifa, Stymie
GLYPHIC	Albertus, Augustea, ITC Barcelona, Bryn Mawr, Congress, ITC Elan, Friz Quadrata, Icone, Meridien, ITC Novarese, Pegasus, Poppl-Laudatio, Proteus, Romic, ITC Serif Gothic
SANS SERIF	
Grotesque	Alternate Gothic, Franklin Gothic, News Gothic, Trade Gothic
Neo Grotesque	Akzidenz Grotesk, Folio, ITC Franklin Gothic, Haas Unica, Helvetica, Imago, Neu Helvetica (numbered series), Univers
Geometric	ITC Avant Garde Gothic, ITC Bauhaus, Bernhard Gothic, Erbar, Futura, ITC Kabel, Spartan
Humanistic	Cosmos, ITC Eras, Formata, Frutiger, Gill Sans, Goudy Sans, Optima, Syntax, Praxis, Shannon, Vela
Square	Antique Olive, Compacta, Eurostile
SCRIPTS	Coronet, Legend, Medici Script, Mistral, Poppl-Exquisit, Snell Roundhand
GRAPHIC	ITC American Typewriter, ITC Benguiat Gothic, Britannic, Draco, Lo Type, Peignot, Pictor, Radiant, Revue

This chart identifies the nine basic type groupings, some of which have been further subdivided for clarity. This chart can be used to help you identify a face, choose the best style for a particular application—or help you in substituting one face for another.

THE ABC'S OF TYPE

Antique Olive

ABCDEFGHIJKLMNOPQRSTUVWXYZ
abcdefghijklmnopqrstuvwxyz
1234567890
$)] - ; / — , . ! ([& - : / ? , . ¢ ¿ ¡ ß £ / — „ ·

ABCDEFGHIJKLMNOPQRSTUVWXYZ
abcdefghijklmnopqrstuvwxyz
1234567890
$)] - ; / — , . ! ([& - : / ? , . ¢ ¿ ¡ ß £ / — „ ·

Antique Olive Light
Antique Olive
Antique Olive Italic
Antique Olive Bold
Antique Olive Black
Antique Olive Compact
Antique Olive Bold Condensed
Antique Olive Nord
Antique Olive Nord Italic

Antique Olive may seem to be a rather silly name for a typeface. Why would anyone want to name a type after a small, oily fruit—especially an old one? Even those who are familiar with type nomenclature may still find the name somewhat odd.

Antique is normally a term used to describe a serif—occasionally a square serif—type. Linking the term *antique* and a sans serif typeface would seem contradictory—except in France. *Antique* is French typographers' nomenclature for sans serif. The rest of the question is cleared up when it is pointed out that Roger Excoffon, Antique Olive's designer, was the design director of the small French typefoundry Fonderie Olive, owned by and named after Marcel Olive.

ATTRIBUTES

Antique is a very big typeface. Outside of a few quirky display designs, Antique Olive has the largest x-height of any typeface you are likely to use. If there is a line of demarcation that separates large x-heights from overly large x-heights, Antique Olive marches up to but does not quite cross that line.

Personality Plus. To further complicate matters, Antique Olive has lots of personality. This is no shy, demure typestyle. It is highly visible, robust, and at times an almost unruly design. It does not look like a conventional sans serif. Antique Olive does not have the geometric overtones of Futura or ITC Avant Garde Gothic. Its shapes do not reflect hand-drawn roman characters as do Optima's; though there are some similarities between it and twentieth-century sans serifs such as Helvetica and Univers, no one would confuse Antique Olive with these types. Because it is a unique design, Antique Olive can be a handful to work with.

Some typefaces, such as Bodoni or Caledonia, have a vertical weight stress. Old Style designs have an obliqued stress on character stroke weights. Most sans serifs

have no apparent weight stress. Once again, Antique Olive dares to be different. Its weight stress is horizontal! It is heavier at the top and bottom than on the sides of its characters. And contrary to most rules of typeface design, the top of Antique Olive is heavier than the bottom. In fairness to this seemingly idiosyncratic handling of character weights, there is a typographic theory that the tops of letters (especially lowercase letters) are the most important to character recognition. Perhaps Excoffon was testing this theory when he drew Antique Olive.

Individual Letters. As a result of its unusual weight stress, some Antique Olive letters (especially the *s*) look like they are upside down. The dots over the *i* and the *j* are also flattened considerably. This was a design necessity (because of the typeface's exceptionally large x-height) to keep the dots within the point body of the face. In the heavier weights, the tops of the *i* and the *j* are scooped out to provide a reasonable amount of white space between the letter and its dot. The *i* and the *j* have benefited from a relatively good solution to the large x-height problem, but the *f* did not fare as well. Its lowered crossbar (again necessary because of x-height) looks awkward and somewhat contrived.

The terminal of the *e* almost touches the crossbar, and the cap *G* suffers from a similar problem in that the right side almost closes up. In both instances, the legibility of the letters suffers. In less than ideal reading conditions, the *G* might easily be mistaken for an *O*. The middle bars of the *E* and the *F* also appear to be too long. Although it contributes to the somewhat eccentric nature of Antique Olive, this trait has no adverse effects on typographic communication. Also, the lowercase *t* is a little out of character: It is the only letter that is based on traditional roman letterforms.

When Caslon was most popular, typophiles would remark that when taken individually, the letters in the face seemed poorly drawn and lacked cohesiveness,

but when set in text composition, everything somehow worked together. The results were generally considered beautiful. Antique Olive meets the first criterion of Caslon, but it does not measure up as well to the second.

Antique Olive is not a bad typeface design; it is just too flamboyant. Flamboyancy can be a contributing factor to graphic communication, but it is not something that is usually sought after.

BACKGROUND

In addition to his position at the Fonderie Olive, Roger Excoffon also ran a flourishing advertising design studio in Paris. Like a surprising number of type designers, Excoffon was a graphic designer first. Typeface design was more avocation than vocation.

Excoffon's types were also primarily drawn for advertising typography, and as a result, they are not confined by the conservative guidelines that dictate the construction of text typestyles. His typefaces tend to be personal—artist's statements—and so lack neither spirit nor verve; you either like them or you do not. (There is little middle ground when it comes to Excoffon's typeface designs.)

Predecessors. Excoffon began his first typeface design just after World War II, but he did not complete this stressed sans, Chambord, until 1951. Chambord is probably the least conventional of Excoffon's designs. It is a relatively straightforward design, distinguished only by capitals that bear a remarkable resemblance to those found in Peignot (an earlier sans serif by another French graphic and type designer, A. M. Cassandre).

Chambord was followed by Banco, a caps-only face that has been described as looking like it was built from bent sheet metal. Banco was followed by three scripts: Mistral, Choc, and Diane. Mistral is by far the most successful of the three and was available as dry-transfer lettering and on two-inch film fonts for many years. Unfortunately, the face is no longer readily available; it's an exceptionally

Antique Olive

Forrest Sigwart of Los Angeles-based Forrest Sigwart Design chose Antique Olive for this ad because it worked well with the face used in the logo design and it made a large body of text type "less intimidating."

powerful (and flamboyant) design.

Excoffon was also responsible for the design of Calypso: the type that answered the question no one asked. Classified as a sans serif, Calypso looks as if it were sculpted out of old scraps of Ben Day screen.

Helvetica's Rival. In 1962, the first face of the Antique Olive family was released. Although planned as a rival for Helvetica and Univers, Antique Olive has emerged as its own, almost unique design statement. It has been called the most striking sans serif since Futura and Gill Sans. Clearly it is—but it is probably not as versatile a communications tool as either of these two earlier designs.

CONSIDERATIONS FOR USE

Antique Olive is not a workhorse text type. It is an important typographic tool and a versatile communicator, but it is not going to replace Helvetica or Times Roman.

Antique Olive's exceptionally large x-height impairs legibility. Character shapes and proportions become less clearly defined than in other, more traditional designs. When set in quantity, this creates a very dark page. Compare a block of copy set in Antique Olive with Times Roman, Univers, ITC Berkeley Oldstyle, or virtually any other traditional text design. The block of Antique Olive will be optically heavier. Antique Olive's ascenders and descenders are reduced to their absolute minimum. The white space produced by more conventional proportions creates a lighter, more inviting page. To compound the problem, Antique Olive's medium weight is bolder than either Univers 55 or the basic weights of Helvetica.

This does not mean that Antique Olive should be considered useless when it comes to setting type in small sizes. It just means that if books, magazines, newsletters, and such lengthy documents as annual reports are the design problems you are struggling with, Antique Olive is not the solution. It may be just right, however, for directories, parts lists, brochures, advertising copy, letterheads, and similar applications, because in small blocks of copy Antique Olive is not plagued by its design's idiosyncrasies—in fact, they may even prove beneficial. The large x-height becomes an asset in short blocks of copy or when information is sought out on a line-by-line basis. If lines of copy are limited to five or six, and ample white space is planned into the page design, Antique Olive does not get the chance to cast its dark shadow.

Antique Olive is an excellent choice for breaking the default status of Helvetica or Univers for parts lists and directories. In these applications, it can be as good a communicator as the more predictable choices, with the added benefit of producing graphic results that have sparkle and distinction.

Bold Display. Even though the text-usage reviews of Antique Olive are mixed, a lot of praise can be directed to this type for display applications. Antique Olive performs all the functions of a display type with ease and grace, and its liabilities for text applications become assets as point size increases. Its large x-height and distinctive character traits make a bold and compelling statement. Antique Olive says, "Read this!"

In addition, most variants of Antique Olive are somewhat condensed. This means that even though the letters are very tall, they do not take up much more space than the standard weights of Helvetica or Frutiger.

Antique Olive is also one of the most gregarious typestyles; it will mix well with almost any other typeface. Like most sans, it will complement virtually all serif types. But unlike other sans serif faces, it will also mix well with its serifless cousins. Most sans serif typefaces share too many similar design traits to work together successfully. (Even mixing a geometric sans serif with a twentieth-century sans serif is a tricky business.)

Antique Olive is technically classified as a twentieth-century sans, but it has such a distinctive design that its mixing capabilities have been expanded to almost universal proportions.

"No Problem" Spacing. Another reason that Antique Olive is potentially a great display face is its remarkable ability to perform well within almost any letterspacing parameters. It can be set "normal," "snug," "tight," "very tight," and even what would be judged by many as "obscene." It is designed so that the sides of round characters (o's, b's, p's, and so forth) are squared off or even a little flat. This allows two of these characters to be set quite close to each other without creating uneven typographic "color" (the texture of a page of type). Antique Olive has the power to produce even color under the most adverse conditions.

A Lesson in Italics. Antique Olive Italic probably is not a very useful design. Italics are not, when the total "type picture" is taken into account, very useful. Studies have proven that they are difficult to read continuously, that readers generally do not prefer italics, and that they are far less effective "attention getters" or "emphasizers" than bold designs. Also, Antique Olive Italic is not much more than an obliqued roman; thus, it is not very distinctive from its upright counterparts.

There are, however, two typographic theories about the design of italic letterforms. One theory holds that simple, obliqued romans make the best italic designs, and that these kinds of designs are most likely to harmonize with and be compared to the basic roman faces. Typophiles of this opinion seek even typographic color and subtle changes in composition through the use of simple, obliqued romans.

The other theory holds that since italics grew out of handwriting, they should continue to reflect and honor the importance of the calligraphic hand. Proponents of this opinion believe that different designs of italic type help the type do its job of standing out on a page and emphasizing important words and phrases.

Both theories are valid, although most italics, and even a few sans serif italics, are designed as cursive letterforms. Antique Olive Italic is an exception. Yet if you believe that italics should be obliqued romans to blend with the upright designs to create harmonious text copy, Antique Olive is still not the face for setting lengthy text copy, and it certainly is not a conservative, mild-mannered book face. It is a face to use when you want something specific noticed.

Availability. Every major typesetting equipment supplier, and most fair-sized type houses, make available a relatively large offering of Antique Olive. The basic design is available in roman, italic, condensed, and expanded variants. There is a heavier weight called "medium" and a lighter version called "light." The light is probably the best suited to lengthy copy, but because it does not have an italic counterpart you are forced (which is good or bad depending on which typographic theory you subscribe to) to emphasize and highlight with bolder designs. Antique Olive also comes in "bold," heavier than medium, and an even heavier design called "compact"; finally, there is the megabold "Nord."

Antique Olive is a finely ground, highly distinctive, and at times rather pungent typographic spice. Used wisely, with discretion, it can add a tasty gusto to your graphic communication. Used too often, however, or in the wrong environment, it can overpower the typographic meal you are serving. Antique Olive is an important ingredient—not daily fare.

ITC Avant Garde Gothic

ABCDEFGHIJKLMNOPQRSTUVWXYZ
abcdefghijklmnopqrstuvwxyz
1234567890
$)] - ; / — , . ! ([& - : / ? , . ¢ ¿ ¡ ß £ / — „ ·

ABCDEFGHIJKLMNOPQRSTUVWXYZ
abcdefghijklmnopqrstuvwxyz
1234567890
$)] - ; / — , . ! ([& - : / ? , . ¢ ¿ ¡ ß £ / — „ ·

ITC Avant Garde Gothic Extra Light
ITC Avant Garde Gothic Extra Light Oblique
ITC Avant Garde Gothic Book
ITC Avant Garde Gothic Book Oblique
ITC Avant Garde Gothic Medium
ITC Avant Garde Gothic Medium Oblique
ITC Avant Garde Gothic Demi
ITC Avant Garde Gothic Demi Oblique
ITC Avant Garde Gothic Bold
ITC Avant Garde Gothic Bold Oblique

There are basically two sans serif type-styles: those that are patterned after the late-nineteenth-century letterforms (Helvetica, Univers, Akzidenz Grotesk, and Frutiger fall into this category); and those that appear to be constructed of basic geometric shapes (Futura, Neuzeit Grotesk, Metro, and ITC Avant Garde Gothic are examples of this).

The ITC Avant Garde Gothic family is perhaps the epitome of geometric sans serif type. It has also become, in the seventeen years since its release, a staple of typographic communication.

ATTRIBUTES

ITC Avant Garde Gothic looks as if it were constructed entirely by ruling pen, compass, and straightedge. As with many things typographic, however, what the eye perceives and what is reality can vary dramatically. Straight lines are obviously straight, but you should know that many of the other, seemingly obvious traits of ITC Avant Garde Gothic are not quite as they appear.

The uniform stroke weight actually is not uniform at all. Horizontal and diagonal strokes are not the same thickness as the verticals; in fact, the weight varies with each group of strokes. In round shapes, the left side or the right side or both are heavier than the top or bottom, and the bottom is slightly heavier than the top. Curved strokes also taper slightly where they join a stem, and the curved strokes that appear to be drawn with a compass are actually carefully constructed and subtly molded hand-drawn curves.

Characters that appear symmetrical are not. A quick tip of the page will reveal that an upside-down S, H, B, and other similar characters are actually bigger on the bottom half than on the top.

ITC Avant Garde Gothic appears geometric because many subtle optical adjustments have been made to the basic character shapes. Typography is a medium governed by optics, and optical illusion is an important aspect of the type design process.

ITC Avant Garde Gothic has a very large x-height, probably as large as a typeface can have before character legibility and typographic readability begin to suffer. (The simple character shapes and exceptionally large counters make up for any deterioration.) A natural result of its large x-height are abbreviated ascenders and descenders.

The display designs of ITC Avant Garde Gothic were released with an extensive set of ligatures and alternate characters. These characters were often used unwisely or to excess, and the late Herbert Lubalin, the typeface's creator, stated that if he had it to do over again, he would not have made these characters part of the design. The ligatures and alternate characters are still available from most suppliers, but they are used less and less often.

Several letters help to distinguish ITC Avant Garde Gothic from other geometric sans serif designs. These also tend (because of their distinctive qualities) to augment the design's legibility; for example, the bowl of the capital R does not close, but the P does, and the cap Q has an almost sensuous curve to its tail—an atypical trait among geometric sans serif styles.

All descenders are abbreviated, but this only becomes obvious in the lowercase g. The crossbar of the capital G also appears to be a little low. Dots over the i and j are rectangular rather than round, and the lowercase a is the single-storied design, the norm for this kind of typestyle.

ITC Avant Garde Gothic was released in two design variations: "text," for use up to about 14 point; and "display," for use in larger sizes. To the casual observer these two designs can appear identical, but there are many differences between the two that make them ideally suited to their tasks. One design trait is not very subtle: The zero in the display design is a full-bodied circle, but in the text it has been narrowed and has flat sides. This design change might seem arbitrary, and the text design might seem a variant to ITC Avant Garde Gothic's normal char-

acter proportions, but tabular material could not be set properly with the display design's varying widths among the different numerals.

BACKGROUND

ITC Avant Garde Gothic started life in the late 1960s as the masthead of the short-lived, often controversial, and always impeccably designed magazine, *Avant Garde*. Herbert Lubalin was art director for this publication, and he conceptualized the magazine logo and its companion headline face. Thomas Carnase and Lubalin were jointly responsible for transforming the idea into a working typeface.

Both Lubalin and the magazine's publisher received numerous requests to release the typeface for general use; however, each was courteously, and firmly, denied.

In 1970, two things happened: International Typeface Corporation (ITC) was formed through the partnership of Lubalin, Burns and Company and Photo-Lettering, Inc.; and *Avant Garde* magazine had ceased to exist. Aaron Burns and Herb Lubalin (principals of Lubalin, Burns and Company) had available a typeface of proven popularity, now free of encumbrances, and a vehicle (ITC) through which to offer the design to the typographic community.

Several months of difficult and labor-intensive work were necessary, however, before the basic alphabet could be transformed into an efficient typeface family. First, many additional characters had to be developed to fill out the various manufacturers' standard character complements. Then a full family had to be built from the basic weights used in the magazine. And finally, each character had to be unitized, and modified many times, to become compatible with text-setting equipment.

Many believe that because of the typeface name and because Herbert Lubalin designed it, ITC Avant Garde Gothic is a new and revolutionary typeface concept. Some typophiles trace its design heritage

Because its products are sold in more than one hundred countries, Adidas has chosen ITC Avant Garde Gothic for its logo, in part for its ease of recognition worldwide.

to the geometric sans serifs produced by Bauhaus designers in the mid-1920s. Actually, ITC Avant Garde Gothic has its foundation in the first sans serif ever produced: a caps-only face issued by the Caslon Type Foundry in 1816. The characters in this design set the standard for the basic geometric shapes found not only in ITC Avant Garde Gothic but in virtually every geometric sans serif produced since 1816.

Initially released as only five roman weights, the family's immediate popularity and the typographic community's continued demands required the release of additional variants. ITC approached Edward Benguiat of Photo-Lettering with a proposal to increase the application range of ITC Avant Garde Gothic by creating condensed designs. These were released in 1974. In 1976, André Gürtler, Christian Mengelt, and Erich Gschwind were commissioned to develop italic versions for this widely used family.

CONSIDERATIONS FOR USE

ITC Avant Garde Gothic can be used equally well for text and display applications. It works for both in a single piece, or it can be mixed with virtually any serif typestyle.

The book weight is perhaps the ideal choice for a variety of lengthy text compositions. Brochures, advertising copy, magazines, and even books have been successfully set in ITC Avant Garde Gothic.

Using the book as a foundation, the demi, italic, and even the bold can be used to highlight and add emphasis. The contrast between book and bold is quite dramatic and, if mixed carefully, can add energy and vitality to many applications.

One of typography's generally accepted rules is that tight, even word spacing produces pages that are inviting and easy to read. From an aesthetic standpoint, the color is improved by close word spacing. A correctly composed text page appears as an orderly series of dark gray stripes separated by horizontal channels of white.

Uneven word spacing not only creates an unsettled and uninviting texture, it also makes reading difficult. In normal reading the eye scans a line, perceiving groups of three or four words at a glance. Word spacing that is uneven or too open forces the eye to read words one at a time. This not only slows down the reading process, it also impairs understanding and retention.

ITC Avant Garde Gothic requires extra attention to word spacing because it lacks the benefits that serifs bring to continuous text copy and because its geometric shapes demand that many letters make only minimal contact with the baseline. Character stress, as a result, has a tendency to become vertical rather than horizontal. Tight, even word spacing counteracts this condition and allows the reader to scan a line quickly and easily.

Text copy in ITC Avant Garde Gothic should be set with tight word spacing, but letterspacing values should be kept within a normal range. Its wide proportions and open counters produce typographic color that tends to be on the light side. An overly tight letterfit can disrupt this color. When set too tight, dark spots occur where characters come close or touch. More latitude is available in larger sizes, but between 8 point and about 14 point, incidentally about the limits for text type, spacing as determined by the type design team should be the norm.

ITC Avant Garde Gothic is an exceptional display face. It attracts attention, is easy to read, and blends well with a variety of text typestyles. An added benefit is that every weight in the family can be combined effectively. The light and medium weights of many sans serif designs do not always lend themselves well to display typography (especially in large sizes); they look weak or ineffectual and have trouble attracting attention. Not so with ITC Avant Garde Gothic—even the lightest weight has a presence and sets with distinction.

Because of its wide proportions, there is also very little design distortion as typeface weights increase. Therefore, even the bold offers exceptionally high levels of character legibility—a claim that few typefaces in this weight range can make.

As opposed to text composition, display copy set in ITC Avant Garde Gothic can be set quite tight—almost touching, in fact. This is again possible because of the inherently high levels of character legibility within the design. Although more latitude is available in intercharacter spacing, the same basic guideline for text composition should also be adhered to in display work; that is, the overall color of the type should be kept even. Dark spots in display typography can be just as disconcerting as in text copy.

ITC Avant Garde Gothic, despite its name, has its roots planted firmly in typographic tradition. It can be applied to a variety of needs and is relatively easy to use. It looks good and wears well. There is also a freshness to the design that belies its age and lineage. ITC Avant Garde Gothic can, and should, be considered a design staple.

Baskerville

ABCDEFGHIJKLMNOPQRSTUVWXYZ
abcdefghijklmnopqrstuvwxyz
1234567890
$)] - ; / — , . ! ([& - : / ? , . ¢ ¿ ¡ ß £/— „ ·

ABCDEFGHIJKLMNOPQRSTUVWXYZ
abcdefghijklmnopqrstuvwxyz
1234567890
$)] - ; / — , . ! ([& - : / ? , . ¢ ¿ ¡ ß £/— „ ·

Baskerville
Baskerville Italic
Baskerville Bold
Baskerville Bold Italic

Baskerville is virtually a one-of-a-kind typestyle. Not only is it the first, and still quintessential, Transitional typestyle, it is also just about the only typeface that fits logically into this classification.

There are other typefaces that can be grouped in the Transitional category, but they are either contemporary copies of Baskerville or typefaces released well over a hundred years after Baskerville was first used. Even these amount to only a handful of designs.

The term *Transitional* refers to the transition between Old Style and Modern designs. William Baskerville's typefaces were both, and they were the first typefaces to break with the design tradition of more than 150 years, and Baskerville's designs directly influenced the work of Fournier, Didot, and Bodoni.

ATTRIBUTES

Baskerville shares design traits with Old Style typefaces and forecasts those of Modern. Like an Old Style, its serifs are heavily bracketed, and those on lowercase ascenders are obliqued. Contrast in stroke weight is more pronounced than in Garamond or Caslon, yet not to the extremes reached by Bodoni and Didot. As in a Modern, weight stress in Baskerville is vertical—gone is the inclined axis of curves found in Bembo or Centaur. It is almost as if Baskerville was created first, and Old Style and Modern typestyles were produced as caricatures, each stressing different aspects of the original design.

"Broad brush" traits help to classify a design, but it is always handy when a particular typestyle has one or two identifying characteristics that are, for all practical purposes, unique to it. With Baskerville's unique trait is the open loop on the lowercase g. Another typical identifier, although less used and therefore less seen, is the capital Q. The tail, which attaches to the main part of the letter by only a hairline, is very robust—almost a full swash design.

The lowercase a has a full counter (the fully or partially enclosed space within a letter) that, along with the other lowercase letters, would normally provide for a high degree of latitude in printing conditions, except that the counter of the e is quite small. This character almost looks out of place with the other full-bodied counters and by itself places certain use restrictions on the family. In keeping with this trend, the e in the italic is also noticeably more condensed than the other characters.

The cap A in the roman has a relatively high crossbar and the J drops below the baseline. The C has top and bottom serifs and the G has just the hint of a spur serif. The lower arm of the cap E is long, and the W has no middle serif.

The general look of Baskerville is quite light and almost (except for the e) full-bodied. In fact, it is said that printers often used Baskerville when they were faced with an expanse of available space and little actual copy.

Until recently Baskerville was available only in a limited family size (in most cases just two weights with corresponding italic designs). When Linotype released New Baskerville in 1978, however, the family size was increased to four weights of roman with complementary italics. This new design has also been subtly reworked to incorporate currently typographic tastes in character construction and proportion; for example, the counter of the lowercase e was made more consistent with the other characters in the face.

BACKGROUND

The Baskerville types are the work of an amateur—in the purest form of the word: They were created out of love, devotion, and dedication. Baskerville, the type, shows a commitment to the process of creating the most beautiful and perfect letterform with no concern for monetary rewards. John Baskerville developed his typeface out of his need to create what he believed was perfect printing. Because he was an exceptionally successful entrepreneur in other businesses, Baskerville did not need to make money from his type design and printing effort. It is a good thing, too, because he would have died a poor man if he had to rely on the typographic trade for a living. The books and types he produced usually found their way into the "red column" of his ledgers.

Baskerville was well past forty when he began to interest himself in typography. The first example of his work (the Latin *Virgil*) was published in 1757. In 1758, he issued a two-volume edition of the works of Milton. In the preface he wrote, "Amongst the several mechanical Arts that engaged my attention, there is no one which I have pursued with so much steadiness and pleasure, as that of Letter-Founding. Having been an early admirer of the beauty of Letters, I became insensibly desirous of contributing to the perfection of them. I formed to myself Ideals of greater accuracy than had yet appeared, and have endeavored to produce a Set of Types according to what I conceived to be their true proportion."

He broke the rules of the typesetting and printing trade to create what he believed was flawless printing and, in doing so, alienated almost all of his contemporaries. He did, however, change the course of typographic development.

It began with his type design. The face he created was light and delicate, more so than previous styles, and it had contrasts in stroke weights that were more pronounced than any current face. Baskerville's type could not be reproduced properly with prevailing printing technology, so he began to improve the technology. He refined the design of the printing press, had paper developed specially for his needs, and invented the hotpressing process. His method of printing was so closely connected with the design and effect of his type that they should not be considered separately.

Unfortunately, John Baskerville was never to know the profound impression he made on the printing craft. Printers and typophiles of the day poked fun at his smooth paper and claimed his light type was unreadable.

Baskerville

Undaunted by such criticisms, Baskerville persisted in the development and use of his type. In fact, in the design, production, and use of his type, he set an example of thoroughness that few have equaled. He worked for more than six years on the design, drawing and redrawing the basic shapes thousands of times. Only when he was completely satisfied did he establish his own type foundry and employ a punch cutter. In the process Baskerville became the first type designer—as distinct from punch cutter.

It would be two more years before his first types were cut, and several more before the first book using them was printed. By 1758, Baskerville had produced eight fonts of type. It was then that he offered his designs for sale and received the rebuff that later caused him to regret the day he entered the printing and typefounding business. Nevertheless, he continued to practice his craft until his death at age sixty nine.

The story of Baskerville's type, however, did not end there. After his death, his wife turned over much of the type to Robert Martin, his senior workman. Four years later, Mrs. Baskerville sold the type and foundry equipment to a publisher for the purpose of printing the works of Voltaire. Fifteen years after his death, Baskerville's type, punches, and matrices were moved to Paris, where they were used for printing during the revolutionary period. Gradually, the type fell into disuse and was passed from one French printer to another until the French foundry of Deberny and Peignot purchased the punches and matrices in 1936. In 1953, Deberny and Peignot presented all the punches to the Cambridge University Press.

From the time of his death until the first part of this century, there was relatively little use of the Baskerville typestyle. Then, in 1910, Stephenson, Blake and Company, the British typefounders, issued a design based not on Baskerville but on a copy of the face released shortly before John Baskerville's death. Seven years later, American Typefounders

Company (ATF) released its version based on the same plagiarized design.

It was not until 1923, when Monotype produced their version of Baskerville, that the work of John Baskerville was faithfully represented. Over the succeeding years several other Baskervilles were released by various type foundries. In 1929, Linotype released a version that had been directly adapted from a font of the type cast mostly from John Baskerville's matrices.

In the late 1960s and nearly 1970s, most manufacturers of photocomposition equipment added Baskerville to their type libraries. The trouble was that they tended to use different sources as the bases for their work. Some used ATF, others used Monotype, and still others used Stempel. To complicate the matter further, differing point-size designs were used as foundations for development. The result was that many Baskervilles were made available to the graphics community with no two looking quite alike.

In 1978, Linotype released their revised and updated version of Baskerville, which not only was a faithful interpretation of the original Baskerville design but also included three additional weights with corresponding italics. For the first time, a true rendition of Baskerville, with a broad range of typeface weights, was available. Four years later, ITC licensed this typeface from Linotype and released it as ITC New Baskerville. At this point, an accurate and exceptionally versatile Baskerville family was made available to the entire graphics world.

Baskerville's typefaces were the catalyst for more than a new style of typeface design; they changed the course of typographic development. If he had merely imitated, or even just improved on his contemporaries' work, there would be little to say about him today. But John Baskerville abandoned tradition and began a movement that was to revolutionize printing and typography of the eighteenth century. Although his faces were not widely used—indeed, they were not even much liked—his typographic arrangements and design style

had a primary influence on the work of Bodoni and Didot.

Baskerville's "unattractive and painful" typeface is one of the most popular serif typestyles in use. It is represented in virtually every type library and can be reproduced on practically any form of type-imaging device. It has become a staple of text typographic communication.

CONSIDERATIONS FOR USE

Baskerville can be a formal alternative to Times New Roman. It has substantially the same vast range of applicability as Times, with only a few cautions to be observed.

Baskerville was originally created as a typeface for setting books. It is therefore ideally suited to the setting of continuous text. Magazines, booklets, brochures, and pamphlets are naturals for Baskerville. It is an exceptionally legible design that, because of its light weight, also benefits from a high degree of geniality. Baskerville is not only easy to read, it is also inviting.

There are only two things to watch for when using Baskerville: The counters in the roman and the italic e can fill if mishandled, and the design, because of its thick and thin contrast, has a minor tendency to "dazzle" (optically vibrate). If a degree of care is taken, however, neither of these potential problems should arise.

Because its serifs are not especially long, and it has generally high levels of character legibility, Baskerville also provides for relatively wide latitutde in intercharacter spacing. Baskerville can be set a little open, or somewhat tight (as long as serifs do not touch), with little loss in its readability.

Baskerville is an elegant design, as becomes quite apparent above 18 point. Baskerville is probably not a face to advertise a circus, but it can be the perfect choice when a sense of formality, grace, or distinction is required.

In spite of its refined, perhaps aloof, appearance, Baskerville gets along well with other typefaces. Old Styles are natural friends: Their somewhat heavy design traits contrast amiably with the delicate features of Baskerville. Kennerly, ITC Garamond, ITC Galliard, and even Century Old Style are great mixers with Baskerville. Virtually any sans serif will also work perfectly with Baskerville. An especially dramatic contrast can be achieved by mixing it with a chunky sans like Antique Olive Bold or Helvetica Black. Another striking combination is Baskerville and a slab serif such as Rockwell or ITC Lubalin Graph. The only instances where Baskerville tends not to mix well is when such typefaces as Caledonia, Electra, or Bodoni are selected. The design traits of these typefaces are too similar to Baskerville's and have a tendency to clash graphically.

If typesetting and printing quality is maintained, Baskerville can be used at small sizes for parts lists, directories, and catalogs. (There is no reason why utilitarian typography cannot be elegant.)

Because of its light weight, typography in Baskerville should normally not be cluttered with ornaments, dingbats, or other graphic flourishes. Rules can be used, but they should be kept simple and confined to a weight no heavier than the character strokes. Also because of its weight, Baskerville rarely is successful when reversed out of a dark color.

Baskerville's heritage as a book face provides it with design traits conducive to a wide range of line-space values. On one hand, its ascenders and descenders are long enough to create a natural white path between lines of text copy that have no additional line space. On the other hand, Baskerville's serifs and x-height are both ample enough for the addition of line space with little loss of reading ease.

Baskerville is an exceptional typeface. It is both elegant and utilitarian, distinctive and legible. It changed the course of printing history and successfully made the transition from metal to photo to digital type. There is only one thing wrong about Baskerville: It is not used enough.

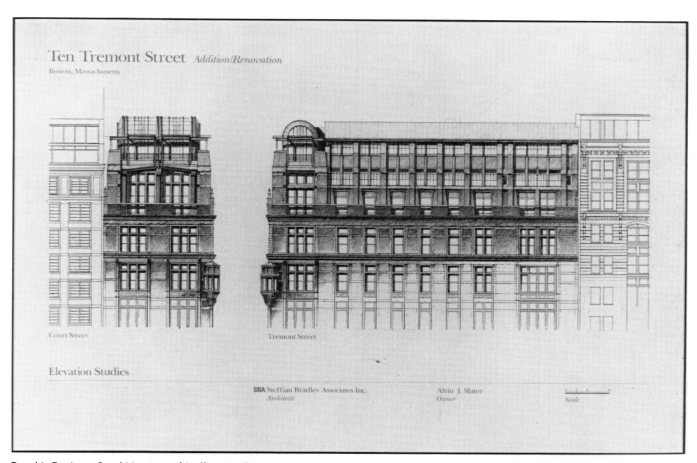

Graphic Designer Boyd Morrison of Steffian Bradley Associates, Inc., an architectural design firm in Boston, selected Baskerville and Univers to convey a sense of duality—a fifty-year-old firm with a modern outlook—for its typographic identity program. Baskerville's built-in elegance and readability is also a boon, as shown on this rendering done for a prospective client.

Bodoni

ABCDEFGHIJKLMNOPQRSTUVWXYZ
abcdefghijklmnopqrstuvwxyz
1234567890
$)] - ; / — , . ! ([& - : / ? , . ¢ ¿ ¡ ß £ / — „ ·

ABCDEFGHIJKLMNOPQRSTUVWXYZ
abcdefghijklmnopqrstuvwxyz
1234567890
$)] - ; / — , . ! ([& - : / ? , . ¢ ¿ ¡ ß £ / — „ ·

Bodoni Book

Bodoni Book Italic

Bodoni

Bodoni Italic

Bodoni Bold

Bodoni Bold Italic

Bodoni Bold Condensed

Typography is normally a logical, straightforward subject, which is why it is even more confusing to many that a typestyle originated in the eighteenth century is classified as a Modern. Perhaps the name came about when typographers realized that the original name for this style of type, Classical, was neither particularly fitting nor accurate. At the time, Modern might have seemed the perfect classification for the most recent style of type.

In any case, the literature of typography has in the past hundred years canonized the term. It would now be considered typographic heresy to change it to a better descriptive.

ATTRIBUTES

Bodoni has become the standard by which all other Modern typestyles are judged. Like most typefaces originally designed for letterpress printing, Bodoni's design traits are directly attributable to technological advancements of the time. Paper stock, which had previously been quite coarse and which forced type designs to be somewhat heavy and monotone in design, had improved markedly in the 1700s. In addition, copperplate engraving became a popular printing method. This encouraged type designs that were imitative of the fine lines the engraver's burin could create.

Bodoni's most obvious design characteristics are its extremely fine hairlines, thick stems, and almost mathematically vertical weight stress. This almost mechanical regularity suggests the use of a ruling pen and compass as the dominant design tools for Bodoni. Capital letters are condensed and serifs are thin, flat strokes with virtually no bracketing. This last trait, very slight serif bracketing, has probably saved Bodoni from typographic extinction. Didot, which was drawn after Bodoni, imitates the engraver's tool to extreme degress. The light strokes are no more than hairlines, and serifs are devoid of any bracketing. Not only does this create a typeface that is often referred to as sterile and rigid, it also creates one that is exceptionally difficult to use well. The visual effect of dazzling is usually the result of trying to set anything other than very short headlines in Didot. Consequently, Didot is rarely used. Bodoni certainly has the same tendency toward dazzling; however, its slightly softened serifs help to offset the condition.

The original type of Bodoni is still used at the Officina Bodoni, a private press dedicated to preserving Bodoni's work, in Italy, but it is restricted to work done just for that office. Although this original is not readily available, an exceptional version of it is. The most faithful revival of Bodoni's original types available today is a face cast by the Bauer type foundry in Germany. In Bauer Bodoni the extreme stroke contrast and perfect vertical stress is easily seen. The Bauer Bodoni *G* faithfully retains Bodoni's extravagant lower serif; the *W* also maintains the double center crossing strokes and the slight separation that occurs between the first and the joined center serifs.

It is in the lowercase that Bauer Bodoni most closely resembles the original. Serifs are slightly bracketed and the top serifs of such characters as *b, h,* and *l* are cupped and not parallel to the baseline. The Bauer Bodoni can also be easily recognized by the slightly curved tail of the *y;* in other designs, the tail is a straight line.

In 1910, ATF introduced Bodoni Book, a lighter version of their earlier revival of Bodoni. This design was not intended to be an actual copy, but rather a rendering that retains the spirit (and much of the basic form) of the original Bodoni type. This design has served as the pattern for the majority of the currently available Bodoni typefaces.

The most obvious (and most beneficial) trait of these Bodonis is the lessened degree of contrast between thick and thin lines, thereby increasing reading ease. This has been accomplished by a weight reduction on the outsides of the letterforms. The result is a design that has acceptable contrast in stroke thickness and slightly condensed proportions while retaining relatively open counters. Much of the objectionable tendency toward dazzling has been removed from these Bodoni designs without altering the original's precise and mechanical flavor. The end products are typefaces that are much better suited to lengthy composition than Bodoni's original was.

Although Bodoni is an easy typeface to recognize, additional characteristics that help to identify it are the serifs at the top and bottom of the capital *C,* the condensed proportions of the *M,* and the vertical tail of the *Q.* The lowercase *g* has a small upper bowl, the lowercase *w* (except in Bauer Bodoni) has no middle serif, and the *c* has a large ball terminal.

BACKGROUND

Giambattista Bodoni has been called "the king of typographers and the typographer of kings." Internationally known and respected in his own time, this Italian type founder, designer, and printer was one of those rare people whose life seems to run according to plan. He was also one of the few people in the typographic arts who became wealthy by virtue of his typographic prowess.

Bodoni was born at Saluzzo in Piedmont, Italy, in 1740. He came to the printing and typesetting arts naturally: His father was a printer. His early childhood was spent at his father's side learning the craft and subtleties of typography. At the age of eighteen, Bodoni moved to Rome to seek his fortune. The first employment he found was as an apprentice to the press of the Propaganda File. Bodoni worked and studied in Rome for ten years perfecting his skills as a printer, typographer, and type designer.

The story is told that in 1776 Bodoni left Rome to visit England, presumably to meet John Baskerville, a man whose work Bodoni greatly admired. But Bodoni never crossed the English Channel. His trip was first delayed by illness.

Bodoni

Then, while he was recuperating, the Duke of Parma persuaded him to manage the ducal printing house. It was here that Bodoni earned the reputation of being the greatest printer of his time. In all fairness, Bodoni was given help in achieving his notability. He had the best tools, equipment, and personnel available; he also had the special luxury of not having to work for clients. Bodoni was, in effect, a completely subsidized private printer, with the enviable opportunity of printing almost anything he wanted.

The new royal printer, upon assuming his duties, continued to use the typeface of his predecessor. He was able to produce some exceptional pieces with this type but soon turned to a face that suited his tastes much better. Baskerville was his choice, and the installation of these new fonts was Bodoni's first major step in his endeavor to change typographic standards.

In 1788 Bodoni cut his first typeface that could be classified as a Modern; others preceded it, but none were true Moderns. At first Bodoni's contemporaries were shocked by the rigid and apparently mechanical shapes, but before the century ended his new design was not only accepted, but admired and copied.

Typographic historians note that Bodoni did not create the first Modern typestyle; he was preceded by several type designers. In 1693 Philippe Grandjean produced a typeface for the French Academy of Sciences at the order of the King of France. Stanley Morison points out that Bodoni's "thin flat serif was foreshadowed two hundred and fifty years before Bodoni was born, namely in manuscripts of the sixteenth century. . . . The thin flat serif can, however, readily be seen in the copybooks of several professional Venetian writing-masters."

Berthold's Bodoni Antiqua has become the standard for IBM-PC print advertising worldwide.

Though not the inventor of Modern type, Bodoni certainly refined the previous examples into a strong and cohesive graphic statement. He also popularized the design and, in doing so, changed the course of typographic history.

CONSIDERATIONS FOR USE

Bodoni is a bit difficult to use well. Its extreme contrast in stroke weight and hairline serifs make for a typeface that is, in many circumstances, difficult to read. When it is used well, however, Bodoni almost always creates a favorable impression. Text copy takes on a refined and elegant flavor, and headlines tend to reflect this same feeling. Some typefaces shout and demand attention; Bodoni speaks in polished tones.

Bodoni body copy can be mixed with a variety of headline faces—sans serifs and Old Style designs work especially well. Headlines in Bodoni are generally most effective when accompanying text is set in the same family. Bodoni does not usually mix well with other Modern typestyles. Their design similarities often create a feeling of discord.

The trick with Bodoni is to overcome its inherent tendency to dazzle on the page. Since the vertical strokes are so dominant and the hairlines so thin, the reader's eye tends to see just the verticals.

The net effect is a picket-fence appearance that optically vibrates. This vibration is exacerbated if the type is set on very glossy paper or in color on colored stock.

First, Bodoni should be set large enough to insure that the hairlines maintain their integrity. Bodoni is not a typeface in which to set captions, directories, or footnotes. It works best at 10 point or larger. In fact, 12 point should be considered over the smaller sizes whenever it is possible.

Text character spacing should also be kept even. This will produce consistent typographic color that, in turn, helps the reading process. There are few, if any, rules in typography that cannot be broken for one reason or another. The avoidance of tightly set Bodoni, however, comes as close to any for being "cast in concrete." Bodoni is just not made to be set tight. Its long thin serifs lock up with surrounding characters, unusual character shapes are formed, and the even, fragile typographic color quickly deteriorates when anything but normal letterspacing is ordered.

Display type can be set tighter than normal and, in some cases, even so tight that letters interweave and interlock. Two things should be remembered, however, when specifying tightly set Bodoni headlines: The result of the final

copy will only be as good as the typographer's skill, and Bodoni tends to lose some of its natural grace and elegance under these circumstances.

Again, to create even typographic color, line spacing should be kept within reasonable limits. Line space should tend to be on the open side. Normal or open line spacing helps to offset the strong vertical emphasis of Bodoni. Most of Giambattista Bodoni's original work with his typeface had a light, airy quality, which was accomplished by generous letterspacing and line spacing.

For best results, column width should also be kept moderate. Very long lines of Bodoni tend to tire the eye and make reading difficult. Using long lines of Bodoni type can create an interesting texture or a graphic effect, but it does not create readable typography.

On the plus side, Bodoni has slightly condensed proportions and is therefore space economical. Even with normal letterspacing, line spacing on the generous side, and relatively short lines, copy set in Bodoni need not take up excessive space.

Bodoni is not an all-purpose typographic workhorse. It is, rather, a high-strung thoroughbred. It is exceptionally beautiful and performs best within a narrow range of functions; but these functions it performs like few others can.

Caslon

ABCDEFGHIJKLMNOPQRSTUVWXYZ
abcdefghijklmnopqrstuvwxyz
1234567890
$)] - ; / — , . ! ([& - : / ? , . ¢ ¿ ¡ ß £ / — „ ·

ABCDEFGHIJKLMNOPQRSTUVWXYZ
abcdefghijklmnopqrstuvwxyz
1234567890
$)] - ; / — , . ! ([& - : / ? , . ¢ ¿ ¡ ß £ / — „ ·

Caslon 540
Caslon 540 Italic

If someone were to say, "Think of a typeface," what would come to mind?

One, two—or maybe three—typefaces would dominate just about every designer's list of first choices. If given much thought at all, however, a larger list would probably result. Even though the typographic spectrum offers a wide and diverse choice of typestyles, only a handful of these tend to dominate in actual usage.

Although currently on few designers' most-wanted lists, Caslon is a dominant typestyle. It has held a position of prominence and been used actively for more than 150 of its 260 years of existence. When you consider that Helvetica has only been around for about thirty years, you get an idea of Caslon's staying power.

ATTRIBUTES

Caslon is classified as a Dutch Old Style type design. (For comparison, Times Roman, Janson, and Plantin are also considered Dutch Old Styles.) As the name implies, Dutch Old Styles originated in Holland.

For much of the seventeenth century, Holland was a major typographic center, producing types for northern Europe and England. These Dutch types were not like the delicate French Old Styles, which preceded them in popularity. They were sturdy designs, with strong, heavily bracketed serifs and a comparatively large x-height. Dutch Old Styles are ideally suited to what used to be called "job work."

The problem with trying to identify specifc character attributes of Caslon is that there are so many different kinds of Caslon designs; even within the general parameters of Dutch Old Style traits, these designs can differ dramatically. The earlier versions (William Caslon's original and its many nineteenth-century revivals) have been called crude and inconsistent in design by typophiles. Character weights and proportions tend to vary from current standards. It is interesting, though, that when these

"crude and inconsistent" letters are combined into words, phrases, and blocks of copy, the overall effect is one of typographic harmony. Later renditions tend to be more refined and technically precise. The resultant typography from these designs retains the inherent beauty of Caslon, though the beauty is subdued when compared to the earlier versions.

Character weight stress in Caslon is normally on an angle, but even this can vary from one design to another. Some Caslons have short descenders, and others are long and elegant. To many it would seem that the only unifying trait among the Caslon designs is the typeface name.

Old or new, refined or crude, all Caslon designs do have one design trait in common: the cropped apex of the capital A. Usually the crossbar of the lowercase e is horizontal and somewhat high; and, almost always, the cap C has pronounced double serifs. Beyond this, there is a lot of latitude.

Less obvious traits include the tight curve to the shoulder of the h, n, and similar characters. The top of the lowercase a also echoes this curve. In many Caslon designs, the R has a subtle curve where the tail meets the bowl. The V, W, and A of the italic in some Caslons appear to be falling over, and the curve that forms the bowl of the italic p usually overlaps the main stroke.

BACKGROUND

Caslon has been called "the oldest living typeface." The original matrices are still available after more than 250 years of service. Original Caslon, just as William Caslon created it, can still be cast in metal from these matrices.

Like many famous type founders and designers, William Caslon did not begin his professional career in the typographic arts. He was an accomplished and prominent engraver before he produced any type. Caslon specialized in engraving and personalizing gun barrels, and his work was highly prized by his wealthy patrons.

Engraving gun barrels would normally not seem to be a prerequisite for designing one of the world's most successful typefaces, yet there were many similarities between this craft and that of typeface design in the eighteenth century. Both demanded patience, artistic ability, skill with engraving tools, and the steady hand of a surgeon. Caslon developed these skills early, and by age twenty four had established his own successful engraving business. In addition to engraving gun barrels, Caslon occasionally took on other small assignments. Silver casting and the production of bookbinders' stamps were two such tasks, which helped develop the skills that would also be useful to him in typefounding.

It is also through the latter two crafts that William Caslon was finally introduced to the typographic arts. John Watts, a successful bookbinder, and William Bowyer, a noted British printer, became aware of young Caslon's artistic ability and engraving skills, and they commissioned his services on several occasions. Watts provided Caslon with his first experience in type design by employing the young craftsman to do lettering and punch-cutting for a number of his book covers. Bowyer added his support by encouraging Caslon to study the art of lettering and typefounding. Later, these two men advanced Caslon the money he needed to establish his first typefoundry.

The basis of Caslon's original roman, and all succeeding Caslon derivatives, can be located in a very humble application. Early in 1720, Caslon was commissioned to cut a font of Arabic type to be used in the publication of a Psalter and New Testament. Printed in 1725 and 1727, this first large typographic undertaking by Caslon, an achievement in its own right, proved to be fruitful in another way. Upon designing the Arabic type he produced a specimen sheet. In order to identify the source of the sheet, he cut a few letters in a roman type (just enough to set the words *William Caslon* as a byline). Perhaps to Caslon the cutting of these letters was a relatively in-

Caslon

significant act, but to those who saw the printed name, it became one of the most important events in typographic history. These few roman letters received so much attention among publishers and printers that Caslon was eventually persuaded to cut a full font of roman and italic.

Thus, William Caslon, just past the age of forty, found himself the owner of the most popular typeface and the proprietor of the best typefoundry in England. His type soon became dominant in other European countries and was even exported to the United States before the American Revolution. In fact, the Declaration of Independence and the Constitution of the United States were both originally set in Caslon.

Over the years, many replicas, recuttings, and attempted improvements of the original Caslon have been produced. One of the first was produced by the Johnson typefoundry in America in the

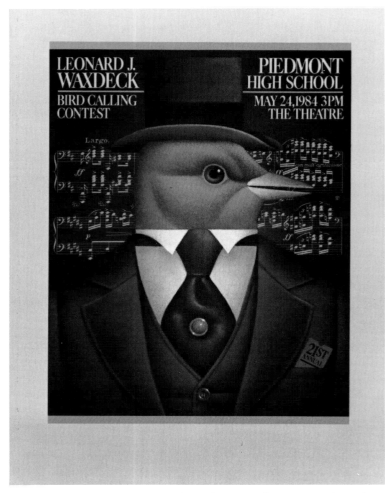

"It's the Rolls-Royce of typefaces." That is the reason designer David Bartels gives for using Caslon in many of his renowned poster designs. As principal of Bartels and Carstens, St. Louis, he created two such designs, incorporating Caslon all-caps display type for the 1984 and 1985 promotions of the Leonard J. Waxdeck Bird Calling Contest. Bartels feels that most Caslon letters can lend themselves to custom-made designing; however, it was not applicable in these cases. The 1984 poster (illustrated by Gary Overacre) and the 1985 poster (illustrated by Alex Murawski) were both typeset by Master Typographers.

early 1800s. This was first called simply Old Style, but the name was later changed to Caslon Old Style No. 471. This design is still available on current photosetting equipment. In 1901, the Inland Type Foundry produced another version, which they called Caslon Old Style. A little later on, ATF released Caslon No. 540, which is also still in use.

In 1916, Monotype introduced a copy of Caslon No. 471 and called their version No. 337. Ludlow copied the same face and called it Caslon True-Cut. Other versions of Caslon are called New Caslon, Caslon 137, American Caslon, Caslon Ad, and Caslon No. 3. Most, however, did not make the conversion from metal to photo type; fewer still are available as digital fonts.

Recently, two new Caslon designs were added to the typographic spectrum: Caslon Buch from Berthold, the German manufacturer of photocomposition equipment, and Caslon No. 224 from ITC. One of the virtues that these two designs have over previous Caslons is that they were conceived and developed as complete type families of coordinated weights. They retain the classic Caslon flavor and look and are firmly rooted in the Caslon tradition, yet they are ideally suited to current typographic standards and output devices.

CONSIDERATIONS FOR USE

Consider the Caslon you are using. Look at the design. There are some general guidelines to keep in mind, but because there is such a variety of Caslons available with such a diversity of design traits, it is difficult (if not impossible) to supply any hard-and-fast rules for this typestyle.

Because of the marked contrast in the stroke width of all currently available Caslons, letterspacing should be kept on the conservative side. Spacing that is too tight will quickly create uneven color in text composition. Moderns and typefaces that tend toward modern design traits need air around characters to help define individual letters and thus promote high levels of readability. (Caslon is not classified as a Modern design, but most current versions begin to approach Modern design traits—at least in the contrast in stroke weights.) As with just about any typeface, word spacing should be tight and even. Putting these two guidelines together, you can assume that Caslon will not work well in narrow columns that are set justified.

The lighter weights of Caslon (Caslon 540 and ITC Caslon No. 224 Book, for example) tend to be more inviting and a little easier to read in blocks of copy than the heavier weights. The thick-and-thin stroke contrast is less apparent in these weights and the picket-fence appearance that causes dazzling is normally avoided.

Most Caslons allow for latitude in line spacing values. Their x-heights are not considered short, as in Bembo or Perpetua, but they are not so large that they demand careful attention. Since Caslon's x-height is moderate, a single point of line space at a 10- or even 12-point setting provides, optically, an abundance of air between lines of type. This helps to make copy set in Caslon look elegant and refined. Because the x-height is not too small, more line space can be added without fear of the lines of type looking disconnected and floating in space.

Caslon is also a great display face. At large sizes, the distinctive (some say idiosyncratic) character shapes become more apparent. Caslon is fun to look at. And all the while, it does not lose its ability to communicate or its beauty and elegance. Caslon at large sizes is rather like an elegant man or woman in formal attire.

Although Caslon can be combined easily with a variety of other typestyles, it does not combine very well with itself. In many cases this is because, outside of the ITC Caslon No. 224 series and Berthold's Caslon Buch, there is no coordinated Caslon family. Both Caslon Old Face and Caslon No. 540 are wonderful text faces, but there is no companion bold designed specifically for either. Caslon No. 3 and Caslon Old Face Heavy can be used, but they are generally too bold, and they do not complement the design characteristics of the lighter faces. With either Berthold's or ITC's design, however, designing in family is an assured success.

Caslon can be contrasted with just about any sans serif typestyle, except perhaps for the lighter weights of Gill Sans. The strong linear and, at times, almost mechanical feel of most modern sans serif designs works exceptionally well with Caslon.

Typefaces like ITC Souvenir, which have moderate contrast in stroke thickness, also are natural contrasts to Caslon. The friendly playfulness of ITC Souvenir, as opposed to the quiet elegance of Caslon, heightens this contrast. Old Style designs like Kennerly and Cloister mix well with Caslon as do many faces, like ITC Bookman or Century Old Style, that have a more vertical weight stress and strong, heavily bracketed serifs.

Although it probably would not work the other way around, text set in Caslon Old Face with running heads set in ITC Lubalin Graph Demi would be a striking combination.

"When in doubt, set it in Caslon" was once a common saying among printers and typographers. This attests partly to Caslon's popularity and partly to its versatility. Although current trends and tastes do not favor Caslon as much as Times Roman or Helvetica, it can be used as an excellent substitute for either of these designs in almost any application.

Century Old Style

ABCDEFGHIJKLMNOPQRSTUVWXYZ
abcdefghijklmnopqrstuvwxyz
1234567890
$)] - ; / — , . ! ([& - : / ? , . ¢ ¿ ¡ ß £ / — „ ·

ABCDEFGHIJKLMNOPQRSTUVWXYZ
abcdefghijklmnopqrstuvwxyz
1234567890
$)] - ; / — , . ! ([& - : / ? , . ¢ ¿ ¡ ß £ / — „ ·

Century Old Style
Century Old Style Italic
Century Old Style Bold

There are differences of opinion about the range of the Century family. Some feel that Century Old Style, Century Expanded, Century Schoolbook, and the various other Century designs are part of one big happy type family. Others feel that each of these Centurys has its own distinct design.

The truth is that most Centurys are related—but not in the traditional sense. When Morris Fuller Benton created Century Expanded in 1900, he drew it as a natural extension of the typeface Century, which his father had produced several years earlier. The Century typefaces that followed it were developed as variations of the same basic structure and proportions, but they did not strictly adhere to design characteristics. Century, then, should be considered as one of the first extended type families.

ATTRIBUTES

Century Old Style is not really an Old Style design. It does have a few Old Style design traits, but they are more hints than a foundation. There is a slight shift in stroke weight stress, but not the strong oblique emphasis found in true Old Styles such as Cloister or ITC Berkeley Old Style. Century Old Style does not have soft rounded serifs, capitals with wide proportions, or even the all-important angled crossbar on the lowercase e— all vital aspects of what has come to be known as Old Style typeface design. It does have, however, angled head serifs in the lowercase and a flavor of Old Style traits—especially when compared to its brothers and sisters in the Century family.

To the neophyte, Century Old Style may be a little hard to identify, but it does have a number of distinguishing characteristics if you know what to look for. Perhaps the most obvious are the large angled serifs on the tops of the capital letters *F, G,* and *T.* This angular serif design is also repeated on the bottoms of the *E* and *S.* The apex of the *A* is angled slightly, and the *G* has a hint of a spur.

Lowercase characters are slightly condensed and almost (but not quite)

vertical in weight stress. In Century Old Style, character terminals are oval-shaped rather than balls, which are found in Century Expanded and Century Schoolbook. The x-height is large, especially for a typeface created more than eighty years ago. The loop and bowl of the lowercase g do not seem to match; in fact, the loop is rather flat looking.

Generally, Century Old Style has more character and personality than the other Century designs. It is the red-headed, freckle-faced member of the family.

BACKGROUND

The first Century in the typographic lineage was released in 1894. It was created as a collaboration of Theodore Lowe DeVinne, one of America's great printer/ typographers, and Linn Boyd Benton, the first president of ATF and father of Morris Fuller Benton. DeVinne considered clarity of text to be of utmost importance in a typeface design, and he felt that the majority of faces available in the latter part of the nineteenth century were far below the quality standards required for a good text face. He approached the young ATF to design a face of greater legibility and readability for his use.

Century Roman was the end result of this effort, and it was first used for the *Century* magazine—hence its name. The face was used in the magazine for several years but not to any great extent by other publications; it was considered by many typographers of the time as too narrow for general use.

One of the younger Benton's first assignments for ATF was redesigning the original Century type, expanding it slightly to be more acceptable for general use. Century Expanded was the result. Without knowing the full story, it can be a little confusing to young typographers to call a typeface of rather condensed proportions Century Expanded.

From that time on, Morris Benton was actively involved in the development of the ATF typeface library. As part of this responsibility he was able to explore many possibilities for developing a type

family. Most of the families he created were developed along traditional lines, in which one set of design characteristics is carried through several variations of weight and proportion. With Century, Benton broke new ground. Here he built his families along similar proportions and structural guidelines, but changed the design characteristics. Where Century Roman and Century Expanded were designed with characteristics similar to Bodoni or Didot, Century Old Style, the next addition to the family, was based on those found in Caslon or Jenson.

In 1915, another dimension was added to the Century family with the release of Century Schoolbook. Designed at the request of an important publisher of school textbooks. the face is a result of exhaustive study on the part of Benton into legibility and readability factors.

Thus the Century family of type is actually three typefaces of distinctly different qualities. They share some basic proportions and characteristics, but they are not as closely related to each other as are the faces within each group.

CONSIDERATIONS FOR USE

Century Old Style should be mixed with care with other Century designs, yet it is a natural complement for many other typestyles. It will mix with virtually any sans serif typestyle and with a variety of serif designs.

Helvetica, ITC Franklin Gothic, or ITC Avant Garde Gothic, especially the lighter or heavier weights, work exceptionally well with Century Old Style. Their almost mechanical structure and minor contrast in stroke weight provide an excellent counterbalance to the obviously roman characteristics of Century Old Style. Not limited to these three styles, Century Old Style can also be used with Frutiger, Futura, or News Gothic. Pick just about any sans serif, and Century Old Style will provide a typographically pleasing counterbalance.

When mixing with serif typestyles, however, a little more care is needed; but even here Century Old Style provides

Century Old Style

lots of latitude. A general guideline is to mix faces not too similar in weight or design characteristics. Typefaces like Caslon and ITC Bookman normally do not mix well with Century Old Style, and faces as diverse as Garamond, Goudy Old Style, or Garth Graphic can all be combined with beautiful results.

Like most typefaces with long serifs, Century Old Style does not take well to tight letterspacing: The letters tend to lock up and either create unfamiliar character shapes or destroy the normally even tyopgraphic color that usually benefits lengthy copy set in this face.

Because of its large x-height (and correspondingly short ascenders and descenders) Century Old Style in lengthy copy has a tendency to look heavy on the page if a little extra line space is not specified. This is not true for all applications, or even for every supplier's version of this design, but it is a potential hazard of which one should be aware.

On the plus side is Century Old Style's ability to withstand less-than-ideal printing conditions and its ability to perform admirably on a variety of paper stocks. Its sturdy proportions, open counters, and the absence of delicate hairlines en-

able it to overcome a variety of hostile typographic environments. Virtually anything can be set in Century Old Style: annual reports, short advertising copy, tabular matter, periodicals, and display headlines. It almost cannot be used in an inappropriate application, and it virtually cannot be overused. Where other typefaces, which have a similar range of abilities, can become commonplace or unexciting (sort of typographic vanilla), Century Old Style maintains a personality and a presence (more like French vanilla). It is an exceptionally versatile, and valuable, design tool.

Fallon McElligott/Minneapolis chose Century Old Style for their *Wall Street Journal* print ads because of the face's classic timelessness and its ability to handle a range of applications well.

The Euterpe
Conservatory
of Music

FRANCIS KEMPTON, *Director*

COURSES are arranged into
three sections, Interpretive,
Vocal and Instrumental. An
unexcelled faculty of noted
musicians insures high
grade instruction

43 Michigan Avenue, Detroit

VOCATIONAL CAMEO

Care and Feeding of
the Infant

SUGGESTIONS FOR THE USE OF
HENKEL PURE FOOD PRODUCTS
ADAPTED FOR THE LITTLE ONE

*NATURE intended children
to live, but the survival is
not the only thing to consider.
To thrive properly and to grow
into perfect robust and healthy
maturity an infant must have
proper foods, suitable clothing
and receive proper care, which
includes keeping the infant as
perfectly sweet, wholesome and
clean as possible. It needs air
as well as the warm sunshine
in abundance and should not*

CLOISTER ORNAMENT

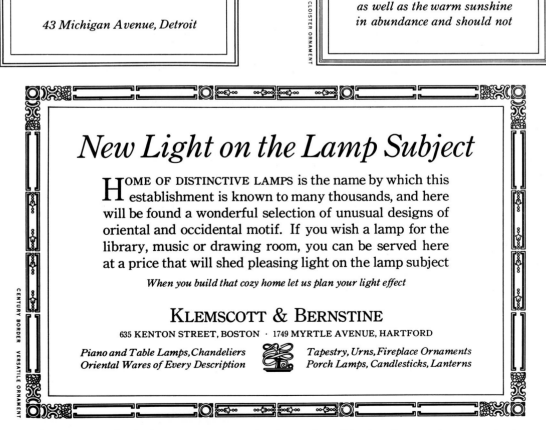

New Light on the Lamp Subject

HOME OF DISTINCTIVE LAMPS is the name by which this
establishment is known to many thousands, and here
will be found a wonderful selection of unusual designs of
oriental and occidental motif. If you wish a lamp for the
library, music or drawing room, you can be served here
at a price that will shed pleasing light on the lamp subject

When you build that cozy home let us plan your light effect

KLEMSCOTT & BERNSTINE

635 KENTON STREET, BOSTON · 1749 MYRTLE AVENUE, HARTFORD

Piano and Table Lamps, Chandeliers
Oriental Wares of Every Description

Tapestry, Urns, Fireplace Ornaments
Porch Lamps, Candlesticks, Lanterns

CENTURY BORDER   VERSATILE ORNAMENT

Century Old Style, in both roman and italic, has a strong personality that works well in virtually any print communication.

ITC Cheltenham

ABCDEFGHIJKLMNOPQRSTUVWXYZ
abcdefghijklmnopqrstuvwxyz
1234567890
$)] - ; / — , . ! ([& - : / ? , . ¢ ¿ ¡ ß £/ — „ ·

ABCDEFGHIJKLMNOPQRSTUVWXYZ
abcdefghijklmnopqrstuvwxyz
1234567890
$)] - ; / — , . ! ([& - : / ? , . ¢ ¿ ¡ ß £/ — „ ·

ITC Cheltenham Light
ITC Cheltenham Light Italic
ITC Cheltenham Book
ITC Cheltenham Book Italic
ITC Cheltenham Bold
ITC Cheltenham Bold Italic
ITC Cheltenham Ultra
ITC Cheltenham Ultra Italic
ITC Cheltenham Light Condensed
ITC Cheltenham Light Condensed Italic
ITC Cheltenham Book Condensed
ITC Cheltenham Book Condensed Italic
ITC Cheltenham Bold Condensed
ITC Cheltenham Bold Condensed Italic
ITC Cheltenham Ultra Condensed

Cheltenham is the typeface we love to hate. Almost no one admits to liking the design. Ask any typophile what he or she thinks of Cheltenham, and you are likely to get a lengthy lecture on what makes the design ungainly, inelegant, and just plain ugly. In fact, if you make the mistake of saying something positive about the face to a group of designers or typographers, you will probably become the target of merciless ridicule and scorn.

And it is not simply current tastes that condemn poor old Cheltenham; no one has gone on record as liking the design since the family was first released in the early 1900s. No one has a good word for Cheltenham and yet someone (in fact, lots of "someones") must be using it. The original Cheltenham ("Chelt" to old-timers) was one of the most successful typefaces of the early twentieth century; and ITC Cheltenham is one of the ten most popular releases from ITC.

Actually, there really is no mystery about Cheltenham. It is a rather homely typestyle, and no one wants to admit to liking something ugly. The other side of the coin is that Cheltenham is an incredibly versatile and effective communications tool.

ATTRIBUTES
Cheltenham is not delicate, it is not elegant, and it is not refined. It is chunky, a little idiosyncratic, and slightly condensed. Cheltenham has no sensuous lines or subtle curves. In its lighter weights, it is almost monotone in appearance. The bolder designs are rich and dark on the page.

One of the first things one notices about Cheltenham is that it is slightly condensed when compared to other designs. This was especially apparent in the metal type. The lowercase letters contrasted dramatically with capitals, which were almost expanded in their proportions. The result was pretty ungainly. In ITC's redesigned Cheltenham, there is an even balance between the proportions of caps and lowercase letters; both are just slightly condensed.

X-Height: The Continuing Argument. Not every typeface requires a large x-height. Many classic book faces perform exceptionally well with modest or even small x-heights. These are styles that, if revised or redesigned for current standards, should not automatically be given a shot of x-height steroids. Cheltenham, however, is not such a design. The original Cheltenham has downright puny lowercase proportions. They do not look elegant like those found in Bembo or sophisticated like those in Centaur—they just look small.

When ITC revived Cheltenham, it increased the x-height. This one design change dramtically improved the aesthetics of the face. ITC Cheltenham is comfortable with its proportions; the design is balanced. In addition, ITC Cheltenham can meet with surprising success in text applications; the original design was never intended to be used at small sizes. A fine novel or a wedding invitation may not be ITC Cheltenham's cup of tea, but newsletters, reports, parts lists, advertising copy, and a variety of other mundane text applications can be perfect for it.

In addition to fixing the x-heights, ITC also performed some major cosmetic surgery on the italic characters of the original design. These were initially created in 1902 to be fashionable or trendy kinds of designs. The difficulty in creating something tendy is that, by definition, within a short time it is dated and unfashionable. The italics of the first Cheltenham are no exception. In the redesign process, ITC made these letters less fussy, less affected, and more usable. They do not look as fancy, but they sure work better.

No one ever claimed that Cheltenham serifs were elegant or sophisticated. They are, in fact, short and a little overweight. Cheltenham's serifs may not be pretty, but they get the job done. They are long enough to aid copy readability and strong enough to survive the worst of printing surfaces.

In the lowercase, many stroke terminals have ball endings. These soften the

design and allow for increased latitude in printing and typesetting conditions. All in all, Cheltenham is a hardworking and very forgiving design.

ITC Cheltenham is easy to recognize in a crowd. Many individual characters give this face distinction and a personality all its own. Perhaps the most obvious is the cap A, which has an apex that extends to the left. It is almost as if the designer drew the stroke too long and then forgot to cut it back. The G has a spur that is quite pronounced in the original design; this is less obvious in the ITC design. The capital E is also a good identifier—its lower arm juts out noticeably more than the top or the middle arm.

In the lower case, the a, g, and s are good characters to look for. The top of the a is not as extended as the bowl; this makes the letter look as if it has a jolly tummy. The loop of the g is an unusual design and does not close. Finally, the s appears to lean forward just slightly.

BACKGROUND
The original Cheltenham is a perfect example of how typeface families were first developed—that is, with almost no planning or forethought.

The idea of a family of type had been around for many years when Morris Fuller Benton took on the responsibility of building the type library of ATF. No previous person or company, however, had taken the concept and developed it to the extent that Benton did.

Benton, a remarkably creative and prolific type designer, also built type families in the manner we are more familiar with today: by designing a series of alphabets that share common traits but differ in proportions, weight, or surface texture. This, however, is where the similarity ends. Today, typeface families are, for the most part, completely planned and organized prior to any font production. Current type families are well thought-out and carefully integrated communications tools. In Benton's time, they grew more like weeds.

ITC Cheltenham

At the turn of the century, typefaces were released first as very small "mini-families" of only two to four designs. These were produced and promoted as a product offering. If the initial offering met with success, additional designs were developed for the family. If these spin-off designs were successful, still more designs could be added to the family. So it was with Cheltenham: From 1902 to 1913, Benton created, and ATF released, twenty-three different Cheltenham designs through this process.

The Original Design. The first Cheltenham, Cheltenham Old Style, was designed by architect Bertram Goodhue for Ingalls Kimball of the Cheltenham Press in New York. The face was originally cut for Mergenthaler Linotype Company, but the rights to recut the type were sold to ATF in 1902.

Benton handled production of the face at ATF, incorporating numerous modifications to the original design. He must have made the correct decisions because Cheltenham became an instant success through ATF. Thus, in 1904, Benton designed Cheltenham Bold and Bold Italic, which were also purchased eagerly by printers and typesetters. In 1905 Cheltenham Bold Condensed was released; in 1906, Cheltenham Bold Condensed Italic, Cheltenham Bold Extended, and Bold Extended Italic were released. By the time Benton was through designing Cheltenham, it was one of the most successful—and largest—typeface families available in America.

From the completion of the family in 1913 until the release of ITC Cheltenham in 1975, the original design never really dropped out of sight. Every printer and typesetter had numerous versions and most were used quite often. Cheltenham did not gather much dust. Still, few professed to liking the design. Outside of ATF promotional material, little was written in praise of poor old Chelt.

In 1975, ITC decided that perhaps they could turn the ugly duckling into a swan—or at least a handsome duck. They initially commissioned Tony Stan to develop just Ultra and Book weights with corresponding italic designs. These were drawn with many subtle (and a few not so subtle) design modifications to the original metal faces. One of the goals of these first ITC designs was to complement the many versions of the first Cheltenham designs, which had been converted into phototype.

ITC soon learned that their designs did not meet their goal of mixability; not because the designs would not mix well with the previous Chelts, but because graphic communicators wanted other ITC versions with which to work—shades of 1902 all over again.

In 1978, ITC succumbed to the many requests from type users and suppliers alike and rounded out their Cheltenham family (but with more forethought than Benton). They developed a weight lighter than the Book and one somewhat heavier. Both of these were also supplied with corresponding italic designs. ITC now had a well-integrated family suitable for a variety of text and display applications. Not altogether satisfied, they also released a full range of condensed designs (eight versions in all) and three display faces (ITC Cheltenham Outline, Contour, and Outline Shadow). With these, the ITC family, at nineteen variations, was almost as large as Benton's original. The ITC design, however, is better sorted out and ultimately a more versatile typographic tool.

CONSIDERATIONS FOR USE

Although it borrows a little from each style, ITC Cheltenham is not an Old Style, Modern, or Transitional design. This means that it will mix well with just about any other typeface. Its rugged features will contrast with the delicacy and grace of Goudy Old Style or ITC Galliard. ITC Tiffany or Bodoni will mix equally well with ITC Cheltenham, although with different results. Body copy in Century Old Style or Times Roman is set off beautifully with ITC Cheltenham heads. It will also combine well with just about any sans serif design, whether the strict geometric forms of ITC Avant Garde Gothic or the more sensuous shapes of Frutiger.

Only typefaces such as Melior or ITC Korinna, which begin to echo some of the design traits of ITC Cheltenham, need to be approached with any cautions. But even designs such as these can be combined with ITC Cheltenham with remarkable success—it just takes a little more care and attention.

Display Type for Text Usage. The original Cheltenham was developed at ATF as a display type family, and usually, good display designs do not make good text faces. Cheltenham was no exception until the updated version also made it exceptionally suited to text composition. The ATF Cheltenham is a fussy design, with a small x-height and capitals that are wide in proportion to the lowercase. ITC Cheltenham has an enlarged x-height, more open counters, and lowercase proportions that harmonize with the caps.

Both the Light and Book weights are excellent for text and are strong enough to stand up to a variety of paper stocks. The Bold will complement either of those designs, and the Ultra, which is really too heavy for much text work, will even provide surprising results if used sparingly.

Because its character proportions are slightly condensed and serifs are on the short side, ITC Cheltenham has a little more latitude than most text designs when it comes to tight letterspacing. Its characters begin to touch much later than other designs, and an even typographic color is maintained within a

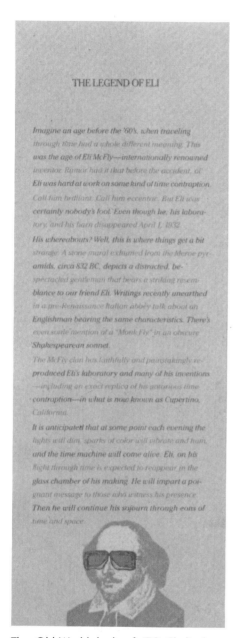

The Old-World look of ITC Cheltenham embellishes the theme of time-travel in Eli McFly's restaurant menu, designed by Rick Tharp and Karen Nomura / Tharp Did It.

wide range of spacing values. ITC Cheltenham is a good face with which to experiment. It is hard to hurt the design.

There are not many condensed serif typestyles, and few of these work very well. Most serif designs are too delicate to withstand the rigors of being proportionately condensed, but not good old Cheltenham. The condensed variants of ITC Cheltenham are exceptionally legible and versatile type designs. It is a good alternative to Helvetica or Univers Condensed, or the lighter weights of ITC Cheltenham Condensed can be mixed with Univers 67 or Helvetica Compact. The results will be distinctive, legible, and surprisingly efficient.

Because ITC Cheltenham is condensed, even in the regular designs, line lengths should be kept on the short side. A long line length will enable you to set many words per line, but it will also have a tendency to tire the eye. A basically lazy organ, the eye does not like having to make too many jumps across a page to gather in bunches of words. Three to four jumps seems to be the eye's comfortable limit. So, when setting ITC Cheltenham, or any condensed design for that matter, line lengths should be kept shorter than normal. But then think of all that wonderful white space of which you get to take advantage.

In text composition, word spacing should always be tight (it helps the eye take in bunches of words rather than having to read them one at a time). This is especially important with condensed typefaces. Word spacing that is too open will not only slow down the reading process, it will also disrupt the natural typographic color of the page. Uneven color is not necessarily a detriment to reading ease, but it is certainly not inviting to the reader. And half the battle of creating effective communication is enticing the reader into the copy. Uneven color is not enticing.

ITC Cheltenham is made for color printing. Because it is a heavy face with moderate contrast in stroke thickness, it holds up remarkably in color printing. Hairlines and serifs will not suffer any loss of integrity, even when printed in relatively light colors.

Along these same lines, ITC Cheltenham can be printed in reverse (light type on a dark background) and over line art with relative assurance that the letters will not dissolve into the background.

How Big? Pick a size, any size, and Cheltenham will communicate with strength and assurance. Because of its sturdy proportions, large x-height, open counters, and distinctiveness of design, ITC Cheltenham can be set exceptionally large. At large sizes, especially in the heavier weights, ITC Cheltenham takes on a lively and friendly personality. Headlines, subheads, advertising copy, even billboards, will benefit from ITC Cheltenham in larger sizes. The only caution is that the heavier weights do tend to work better at these larger sizes than the lighter designs of ITC Cheltenham. In the Book and Light weights, the short serifs and optically monotone stroke weights tend to make the face look plain. These versions can be used in larger sizes, but some of the spark and vitality, so apparent in text settings, begins to be lost. Save the light weights for sizes below 18 point.

The majority of the design community will probably continue to profess hating Cheltenham for some time to come. Traditions die hard. There has always been some leeway between what people say and what they do. So as long as the typestyle continues to be used actively, and with good taste, it probably does not matter too much what is said about the design, because no matter how much we love to hate Cheltenham, it really is a very good face.

ITC Galliard

ABCDEFGHIJKLMNOPQRSTUVWXYZ
abcdefghijklmnopqrstuvwxyz
1234567890
$)] - ; / — , . ! ([& - : / ? , . ¢ ¿ ¡ ß £ / — „ ·

ABCDEFGHIJKLMNOPQRSTUVWXYZ
abcdefghijklmnopqrstuvwxyz
1234567890
$)] - ; / — , . ! ([& - : / ? , . ¢ ¿ ¡ ß £ / — „ ·

ITC Galliard
ITC Galliard Italic
ITC Galliard Bold
ITC Galliard Bold Italic
ITC Galliard Black
ITC Galliard Black Italic
ITC Galliard Ultra
ITC Galliard Ultra Italic

Computer technology has invaded the craft of typeface design, once the exclusive realm of age-old tools and time-honored techniques. Now design software, video terminals, and electronic plotters are becoming active contributors to the process of typeface design.

With change there is uncertainty; and unfortunately, with uncertainty there is too often fear. One of the more commonly voiced fears of this particular changeover is that the end results will lack the warmth and grace (the humanity) of previous designs. ITC Galliard contradicts this assumption.

One of the first original typefaces to be created through extensive use of computer technology, ITC Galliard is a type that is as beautiful, elegant, and vibrant as any created through more traditional means.

ATTRIBUTES

Most modern typeface designs cannot be pigeonholed into traditional type categories; ITC Galliard is one such face. It fits neatly into a classification shared by typefaces many years its senior. This is because it is a revival design, a modern version of an existing typestyle. Both Matthew Carter, the type's designer, and Mike Parker, its editor and art director, studied the antique type housed at the Plantin-Moretus Museum in Antwerp. Both came to the conclusion that the graphic community would benefit from a modern version of the typical typeface used during the northern European Renaissance. Today these typefaces are referred to as Dutch Old Style.

These types are distinguished from their close Aldine predecessors (Garamond, Bembo) by their marked contrast in stroke weight and large x-heights. Typophiles postulate that these characteristics are a result of melding Garamond's design traits with the black letter types common to northern and central Europe.

Personality Plus. ITC Galliard has been called exuberant, baroque, vibrant—and

even sensuous. It is probably all of the above. This is a typeface with exceptional verve and vitality. Its character strokes are strong, sure, and slightly flamboyant. If one character were chosen to characterize the design, it would be the lowercase italic g; firmly based in Dutch Old Style typographic tradition, it is also as vital and lively as any calligrapher's brushstroke.

The bolder weights of ITC Galliard have personality without being mere caricatures of the lighter designs. In addition, they have a strength not found in most heavy typefaces. Where faces like Bramley Extra Bold and ITC Souvenir Bold look like Lou Costello, ITC Galliard Ultra has the strength and muscularity of an Arnold Schwarzenegger. The Black and Ultra weights of ITC Galliard are as powerful and aggressive as any display faces you will likely use.

The serifs of ITC Galliard are also strong. Long and heavily bracketed, they give substance to the design and improve readability when the face is used appropriately. Like Plantin, Caslon, and Times Roman, its Dutch Old Style brethren, ITC Galliard has angled head-serifs, which look like little banners attached to the vertical strokes. Also like Caslon and Plantin, the apex of the capital A in ITC Galliard has a distinctive treatment. In Caslon, it is cupped. In Plantin, the bold stroke overlaps the hairlines. ITC Galliard has a little bit of both.

Other characters that help to distinguish ITC Galliard are its P, which has a bowl that does not quite close; its unusual splayed italic Y; and the a, which has a distinctive top terminal. Equally distinctive, but perhaps less apparent design attributes are the nonattached diagonals of the cap K and the extended diagonal of the N.

BACKGROUND

The idea to design Galliard came from Mike Parker and probably originated as early as 1958 (well before computers had any effect on typeface design). In the late

1950s, prior to becoming director of typographic development at Mergenthaler Linotype, Mike Parker was deeply involved in a research project, studying the antique punches and matrices housed at the Plantin-Moretus Museum in Antwerp. The work of Robert Granjon was part of this typographical treasure to which Parker was exposed.

Granjon was a Parisian, born approximately a generation after Claude Garamond. An exceptionally talented and prodigious type designer, he also had an incurable case of wanderlust. He traveled throughout Europe, working on various design commissions within a particular city and then moving on to other commissions in other cities. Wherever he went, Granjon planted the seeds of his typographic style (sort of the Johnny Appleseed of type).

Granjon worked in Antwerp in the late 1560s and left behind the beautiful types that stole Mike Parker's heart. It became one of Parker's many desires to make these wonderful antique letters, unused for so long, available to the modern design community. The problem was that Mike Parker is not a type designer. Over six years passed before his dream began to take physical form.

In 1965, Matthew Carter, a remarkably gifted type designer, and also a big fan of Granjon, joined Mergenthaler Linotype. All the ingredients were in place: passion, talent, manufacutirng, and marketing resources. With an eye toward satisfying both the typographic purist and Mergenthaler's controller, Carter and Parker set as their goal producing the best possible Granjon type for contemporary typography. In Carter's words, "The object of designing Galliard was to make a serviceable, hard-working, adaptable, contemporary, photo-composition typeface based on a strong historical style. . . . The result is not a literal copy of any one of Granjon's faces, more a reinterpretation of his style. The face was produced by drawing from scratch rather than working over enlarged photographs of punches or proofs."

ITC Galliard

Matthew Carter created the Roman and Black weights of the series and all the italics through very traditional means. The Bold and Ultra, however, were created through computer technology. For this he called on the services of a small software house in Hamburg, Germany. URW and their Ikarus software are now famous throughout the type design community, but they were just getting started when Carter first took advantage of their capabilities. The Ikarus software was not nearly as powerful then as it is today, and it was only used to electronically interpolate the Bold designs and then to extrapolate the Ultra. This was just the first of many typefaces to be developed with the aid of computers. Faces such as Garth Graphic and Shannon from Compugraphic, Eldorado and several other new designs from Linotype, and most recently, the ITC Stone type family released by Adobe Systems, were all created using computer technology as a design tool.

Galliard was released by Mergenthaler Linotype in the winter of 1977–78 and released by ITC as ITC Galliard through a licensing agreement with Linotype in 1981.

Paul Curtin of San Francisco's Paul Curtin Design chose ITC Galliard for these National Fitness Campaign brochures for two reasons: "It had to appeal to our market on a sophisticated corporate level and communicate honestly to schools and community."

CONSIDERATIONS FOR USE

Tired of using Times Roman? Want to cut down on your intake of Garamond? Like a change of pace from Century Schoolbook? Try ITC Galliard. Just about any application that can be fulfilled through the use of standard and predictable typefaces can be satisfied equally well with ITC Galliard. This revived Granjon does, however, have its own personality, and this must be contended with to produce optimum results.

ITC Galliard is a strong design. It is a little on the heavy side, just slightly heavier than Baskerville or Goudy Old Style. In addition, it begins to show the contrast in stroke thickness found in its Transitional and Modern cousins. The good news here is that it will survive adverse printing and reading conditions better than its more delicate relatives. ITC Galliard stands up to a variety of paper stocks. It will also hold color well; its main strokes are strong enough to provide adequate contrast between colored type and its background. Its hairlines are thin, however, so it is not a face to reverse out of a dark background.

Because of its slightly stronger stroke weight, ITC Galliard will make a more substantial statement than many more traditional choices. A block of text copy set in it will be darker than text set in Goudy or ITC Berkeley Old Style, but not quite as dark as Times Roman. These are subtle differences, but they can be important when you are trying to create just the right "feel" or "look" for your page.

The Importance of White Space. ITC Galliard likes a little elbow room. Give it enough intercharacter and interline spacing. It has full, richly bracketed serifs, which help when it comes to typeface readability but which can also work to its detriment if letters are spaced too close together. If tight letterspacing is ordered, the individual letters will begin to lock up with their neighbors. This causes dark spots in what should be evenly colored text copy. Initially, these dark spots look ugly, and, perhaps more important, they draw the eye away from the normally smooth and orderly reading process. The first concern is cosmetic, the second, pragmatic. If you do not mind ugly copy, that is your business; but copy that is difficult to read is everybody's business.

That is fine for text copy, where generous interletter spacing is easy to live with, but what about headlines and such? Matthew Carter foresaw this problem and solved it. He drew the serifs proportionally shorter as the family weights go bolder. This allows them to be set tighter for headlines and other display copy. (Not every type designer takes such good care of graphics people.)

Although you do not have to be nearly as careful, the white space between lines of type also needs a little attention. ITC Galliard works just fine right out of the box; but ordering negative line space from your typographer will only result in a block of copy that looks too dark. This is another cosmetic problem that really does not hurt copy readability—until ascenders start touching descenders. However, studies have shown that people tend to read copy that is light and inviting (especially if subheads and other visual stimuli are supplied) over copy that is presented as heavy or dark texture.

Line and Alphabet Length. ITC Galliard's thick and thin contrast in stroke weights calls for column widths that are not too long (about eleven or twelve words is fine). This face has just the slightest tendency to dazzle. Shorter line lengths tend to counteract this potential problem.

Because it is slightly more expanded than Times Roman, ITC Galliard is probably slightly more legible. The good news is that this increase in character expanse, although visually apparent, has little effect on copy count. The lowercase alphabet of ITC Galliard is only slightly longer than that of Times Roman, another virtue of clever and talented typeface design.

Italics are the butterflies of typography. They are charming, beautiful, and graceful but not terribly utilitarian. Most experts agree that italics do not make very good emphasizers, and they are difficult to read in lengthy copy. The italics in ITC Galliard, however, come very close to overcoming these handicaps. They are exceptionally vibrant and distinctive (which makes them wonderful emphasizers), and they are surprisingly easy to read. The only drawback is that the bolder weights, in larger sizes, tend to look fussy. The bottom line? Use ITC Galliard's italics to your heart's content—just not for display headlines.

Accessories. ITC Galliard, like a Japanese car, comes "fully loaded" from the factory. It has one of the most extensive ranges of complementary and support characters: Old Style figures, ligatures, small caps (in two weights), and even a handy set of alternate and swash characters for display work are included in the basic offering. Take advantage of these typographic niceties. Order ligatures; they not only read better than their nonconnected counterparts, they also look classy. Use the Old Style figures in text copy. This is what they were designed for, and ITC Galliard's perform their tasks admirably. Small caps can be versatile typographic tools. Use them, but do not accept electronically produced substitutes. Finally, use the swash and alternate characters—but not too much.

With one serif firmly planted in the tradition-bound world of Robert Granjon, and another in our current world of design software, ITC Galliard successfully spans the gaps of time and technology. The design was well planned and exceptionally well executed. The result is a type family that is versatile, powerful—and even a little sexy.

ITC Garamond

ABCDEFGHIJKLMNOPQRSTUVWXYZ
abcdefghijklmnopqrstuvwxyz
1234567890
$)] - ; / — , . ! ([& - : / ? , . ¢ ¿ ¡ ß £ / — „ ·

ABCDEFGHIJKLMNOPQRSTUVWXYZ
abcdefghijklmnopqrstuvwxyz
1234567890
$)] - ; / — , . ! ([& - : / ? , . ¢ ¿ ¡ ß £ / — „ ·

ITC Garamond Light
ITC Garamond Light Italic
ITC Garamond Book
ITC Garamond Book Italic
ITC Garamond Bold
ITC Garamond Bold Italic
ITC Garamond Ultra
ITC Garamond Ultra Italic
ITC Garamond Light Condensed
ITC Garamond Light Condensed Italic
ITC Garamond Book Condensed
ITC Garamond Book Condensed Italic
ITC Garamond Bold Condensed
ITC Garamond Bold Condensed Italic
ITC Garamond Ultra Condensed
ITC Garamond Ultra Condensed Italic

There is only one Helvetica, only one Times Roman, one Optima, and only one Univers. Each type supplier may have its own version of these faces, and their names may change from one company to another, but the bottom line is that the end product (the design) is essentially the same, no matter where you get it.

Not so with Garamond. There is an ATF version of Garamond, a version developed by Lanston Monotype, one produced by English Monotype, and another drawn for Simoncini. Linotype has two versions (three if you count the Stempel design).

Most current suppliers offer at least two different versions of Garamond, and they all offer ITC Garamond, the newest addition to the Garamond family of type. Each verison of Garamond has its own, distinctly different typeface design. When talking about Garamond it is important to know which version you are discussing.

ATTRIBUTES

There are many different Garamond typefaces, but they all are classified as Old Style designs and therefore share a number of similar design traits. First, the character weight stress is angular, with the heaviest stroke at approximately the two and eight o'clock positions. Head serifs are triangular, and all serifs tend to be long with soft rounded ends.

Other typical Old Style traits common to Garamond are a small bowl on the lowercase *a* and a high crossbar on the *e*. One other trait that just about every Garamond shares is the "bidirectional" serifs on the top of the cap *T*. They can all also be referred to as graceful and elegant typeface designs.

As for the differences, even though the variations can be quite dramatic from one Garamond to another, all Garamonds tend to fall into two categories: American and European.

The American design style of Garamond is the first twentieth-century revival of the Garamond types. These faces, exemplified by ATF's Garamond, Lino-

type Garamond No. 3, and ITC Garamond, tend to be softer designs with larger x-heights than the European versions. Stempel Garamond and Simoncini Garamond typify the second group. In these faces, contrasts in character stroke width tend to be more pronounced, x-heights are on the smallish side, and letters appear more angular, as if they were drawn with a chisel-point pen or brush.

Comparing the lowercase *a* in ITC Garamond to that in Stempel Garamond provides a concentrated view of the design differences between the American and European typestyles.

BACKGROUND

Claude Garamond is generally credited with establishing the first typefoundry. He was the first type designer to create faces, cut punches, and then sell the type produced from the punches. Unfortunately, Garamond also had little success in this business. He died owning little more than his punches, and shortly after his death in 1561 his widow was forced to sell these.

Garamond was not personally successful, but his typefaces certainly were. Eventually, they were used throughout Europe. They found their way to Holland via Christopher Plantin; to Germany through André Wechel, the executor of the Garamond estate; and into Italy via Guillaume Le Bé, one of Garamond's students. Garamond's work was emulated and copied in most of literary Europe. In France, his work became a national style; his punches were used to inspire the creation of many fonts of type. Some of his punches were even identified as part of the original equipment of the French Royal Printing Office, established in Paris by Cardinal Richelieu, almost a hundred years after Garamond's death. Richelieu used the type, referred to as the "Caractères de l'Université," in the printing of his book, *Les Principaux Poincts de la Foy Catholique Défendus*. It's on this type that most modern Garamonds are based.

One of the first, Morris Fuller Benton's design for ATF in 1919, met with almost

instantaneous success. The other major foundries brought out their versions in quick succession. In 1921, Frederic Goudy completed Garamont, a similar design inspired by the same source, for Lanston Monotype. The English Monotype Company followed in 1924 with its own interpretation of Garamond, again inspired by the Caractères de l'Université. Once again the Garamond designs were immensely popular.

In 1926, however, a lengthy and thoroughly documented article by Paul Beaujon in the *Fleuron* established that Jean Jannon designed the type on which these later Garamonds were based more than eighty years after Claude Garamond's death. Jannon was a printer and punch cutter in Paris. Early in his career he came into contact with, and was obviously impressed by, the original work of Garamond. In the early seventeenth century, Jannon's Protestant sympathies took him to Sedan, north of Paris, where he worked in the Calvinist Academy. Because he had difficulty securing materials for his work, he made many of his own. Over a period of time, friction between Jannon and the authorities in Sedan resulted in his return to Paris.

Jannon took his type and punches with him, and he worked for only a short time before his religious leanings got him into trouble again. Jannon was forced to leave Paris but not before his type and punches were confiscated by the government. These eventually found their way into the French National Printing Office, where they were used by Cardinal Richelieu. The type was then placed in the Printing Office archives, where they remained in obscurity for over two hundred years.

In 1845, the type was rediscovered and brought out for use by the Imprimerie National at Paris, which, two years later, printed two specimen books showing the type and attributing it to Garamond. At the turn of the century, the director of the French National Printing Office studied the available material and announced that, indeed, the type was the work of Claude Garamond.

ITC Garamond

Paul Beaujon discovered a specimen book of Jannon's in the Mazarin Library in Paris, and through careful and exhaustive research he was able to prove that Garamond types residing in the French National Printing Office were actually the work of Jannon. This revelation—a sensation in the typographic world—perhaps was equalled only by the revelation that "Paul Beaujon" was actually Beatrice Warde writing under a pseudonym. At the turn of the century, printing and typography was a "man's business," and Warde must have felt that no one would believe the theories of a woman. But this woman went on to become a major force at the English Monotype Company and one of the most celebrated historians of the typographic arts. Few have surpassed her accomplishments.

Meanwhile, other Garamond designs were created based on the type actually produced by Claude Garamond. George Jones, of England, created a design based on the original Garamond in 1924. It was released by Linotype and Machinery, London, and for some unknown reason was not named Garamond, but Granjon, after a contemporary of Garamond. In 1925, both Mergenthaler Linotype and Stempel released designs based on the actual type of Claude Garamond.

The Fleuron article did much to advance the popularity of the Jannon-based Garamond designs. In fact, they became so popular that other foundries duplicated the style; Intertype in 1927, Mergenthaler Linotype in 1936, and even Monotype in 1938. The Linotype version is called Garamond No. 3, and the Monotype is called American Garamond, to distinguish them from earlier designs.

Finally, over a period of five years, ITC released a large Garamond family of sixteen designs, which brings the design concept full circle. ITC Garamond was created as a harmonious family of faces, in which all three variations are balanced contributors.

Thus, the irony: that the designs of an unsuccessful type designer, who died virtually penniless, would influence the design of a score of typeface families bearing his name; and that the various versions would account for some of the most consistently popular typestyles of the last seventy-five years.

CONSIDERATIONS FOR USE

The varied styles of Garamond may be a little confusing, but they are all easy to use and have virtually no limits to their range of applications.

Garamond in both the American and European styles is generally considered to be the quintessential book face. There was a time, B.T.R. (Before Times Roman), when most fine books were set in a Garamond type. And if it is good for books, then Garamond is also an excellent choice for most other forms of continuous text. Magazines, newsletters, annual reports, lengthy advertising copy, and similar applications are all naturals for Garamond. Grace, elegance, readability, and legibility are the benefits.

Any typeface ideally suited to lengthy copy can also be used with equal success in short blocks. (Unfortunately, the converse is not true.) If it can be set in type, it can probably be set, with good effect, in Garamond. Even parts lists, directories, and other applications that normally call for a condensed design can benefit from Garamond's elegance—if one of the condensed designs of ITC Garamond is used.

The only limits to Garamond's use come with the European versions. Because of their higher contrast in stroke thickness and smaller counters, these must be used with some care and discretion, especially in smaller sizes and when printed on textured paper stock. Even these, however, have surprising latitude in their range of applications.

Just about every Garamond mixes well. Sans serifs are a natural; the soft edges and fine curves of Garamond contrast beautifully with the hard edges and

Classic yet modern, ITC Garamond offered the range of weights and the readability Time, Inc., needed for its 1986 annual report, designed by Gips + Balkind + Associates, Inc./The GBA Group.

geometric shapes of sans serifs. And practically any sans serif will do. From the strikingly humanistic designs of Frutiger to the geometric ITC Avant Garde Gothic, there are few limits to Garamond's flexibility when it comes to sans serifs.

Garamond's friendliness extends equally well to serif typestyles. Typefaces with vertical (or nearly vertical) weight stress, obvious contrast in stroke thickness, crisp edges and well-defined serifs, or strong calligraphic overtones all mix exceptionally with Garamond. From Century Old Style to Clarendon, Times Roman to ITC Tiffany, Icone to ITC Lubalin Graph, and everything in between, Garamond complements and contrasts with a variety of serif typestyles. The only designs that might pose problems are those with very similar design traits. Garamond and Bembo, or Garamond and Goudy Old Style, for example, may be difficult to combine.

Even though it is classified as an Old Style design, Garamond need not be confined to traditional or conservative uses. Apple Computers has used ITC Garamond as its corporate typeface, and Apple's ads are knwon for their fresh, lively quality. AT&T also uses ITC Garamond for its Bell Laboratories ads, as does Kawasaki for its motorcycles. Garamond can be just as current as an ITC Avant Garde Gothic or Helvetica.

The ITC version of Garamond also allows you to "design in family," thereby adding continuity to lengthy or complicated pieces. In addition, ITC enlarged the x-height of their design over previous versions. This design trait both improves legibility and readability levels, with the slight drawback that leading should be watched a little more carefully in text composition than with other Garamonds, to ensure even color and sufficient optical line spacing.

One last note: None of the Garamonds takes well to exceptionally tight letterspacing. It ruins the even and inviting typographic color naturally created by this style.

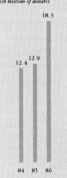

INSTRUCTION
OPERATING REVIEW

INSTRUCTION
OPERATING INCOME
(in millions of dollars)

18.3
12.4 12.9

84 85 86

GUMP'S

{20}

MACMILLAN'S instruction businesses in 1986 achieved operating income of $18.3 million, a 42% increase over 1985, on sales of $159.4 million. Teaching skills that range from languages to office procedures to technical trades, these businesses continue to adapt and grow with the changes that information technology has brought to their respective markets.

BERLITZ. Increased demand for English instruction in Europe and Japan helped Berlitz achieve another excellent year in 1986, with operating income increasing 67% on sales growth of 37%. Long the premier name in foreign language instruction throughout the world, Berlitz continues its success in developing new products. In 1986, these included a revised series of phrase books for travelers and a new program called Berlitz, Jr., in which Berlitz, under contract with elementary schools, provides small-group instruction in foreign language conversation to children in kindergarten through grade six. This modified form of the Berlitz method has proven highly effective in teaching young children, who can learn new linguistic skills more easily than older persons can. Market demand for the product has far exceeded projections, and it is anticipated that Berlitz, Jr., will become an important part of Berlitz's revenue stream in the coming years.

KATHARINE GIBBS. With a unique curriculum that combines traditional administrative skills with the latest in office automation, Katharine Gibbs continued its 75-year leadership in office skills instruction. Significant achievements during 1986 included the development of three new curricula—travel and conference planning, hotel and restaurant management, and accounting—that are currently offered at selected Gibbs campuses. Gibbs also experienced significant revenue growth from its Continuing Education programs in 1986.

TECHNICAL SCHOOL DIVISION. The Technical School Division grew in 1986 with the acquisition of Wyoming Technical Institute, which offers training in automotive and diesel technology. Other achievements in 1986 included the development of nursing assistant training and hotel and restaurant management programs at The Stone School and the development of a computer peripheral repair program at the Technical Careers Institute.

While other retailers live—and die—by following trends, Gump's has adhered to an unchanging style of retailing that has earned it a loyal following among upscale customers. In 1986, Gump's achieved increased revenues and operating income from sales at its four retail stores and through the Gump's Gift Book.

The classic elegance of Garamond No. 3 reflects the feeling of stability and confidence Macmillan, Inc., wanted to convey in its 1986 annual report, designed by Gips + Balkind + Associates, Inc./The GBA Group.

Gill Sans

ABCDEFGHIJKLMNOPQRSTUVWXYZ
abcdefghijklmnopqrstuvwxyz
1234567890
$)] - ; / — , . ! ([& - : / ? , . ¢ ¿ ¡ ß £ / - „ ·

ABCDEFGHIJKLMNOPQRSTUVWXYZ
abcdefghijklmnopqrstuvwxyz
1234567890
$)] - ; / — , . ! ([& - : / ? , . ¢ ¿ ¡ ß £ / - „ ·

Gill Sans Light

Gill Sans Light Italic

Gill Sans

Gill Sans Italic

Gill Sans Bold

Gill Sans Bold Italic

Gill Sans Extra Bold

Gill Sans Extra Bold Condensed

Gill Sans Ultra Bold

Gill Sans Ultra Bold Condensed

Most sans serif typestyles work like ballpoint pens: They are reliable communications tools that require little care, and they provide predictable results. The line produced by such a pen lacks any form of personality, but one does not usually hold high expectations for it. In terms of results, Helvetica can be compared to a ballpoint pen. Gill Sans, however, works like a sable brush.

ATTRIBUTES

Gill Sans has often been called "the most civilized of sans serif typefaces," because its design foundation is in roman letterforms and proportions. There is no T-square precision, nor are there geometric shapes, in Gill Sans. This typeface is clearly the result of a calligrapher's hand. In fact, the punch-cutters at Monotype Corporation who were responsible for converting the drawings of Eric Gill, a calligrapher and stone carver, into metal type felt that there was too much calligraphy in the design as it was originally proposed. A comparison of Gill's submitted renderings and the completed design reveals that the final product is more structured than what the original artist intended. The Monotype technicians were attempting to remove some of the idiosyncracies that perhaps made the typeface more interesting but also less utilitarian.

Fortunately, the Monotype punch-cutters did not sterilize the design in the process of making it a useful typographic tool: The hand of the artist-calligrapher is still very apparent. The fact that Gill Sans is not (like most sans serif types) based on geometric proportions makes it stand out from the crowd. Even at a glance, Gill is different from other serifless faces. This can be a benefit or a drawback, depending on how the face is handled. Just remember that this is not just another sans serif type.

Smaller Can Be Better. Gill has a relatively small x-height—smaller than Futura and a lot smaller than Helvetica. In today's world of large x-heights, Gill's diminutive size may seem to be a typographic drawback. This need not be the case: First, Gill's individual letters are exceptionally legible; second, since there is more of a pronounced contrast in stroke width in Gill Sans than in most other sans serif typefaces, it is more readable than its typographic cousins. An added benefit is that more information can usually be set in a given space when using Gill than when using most other sans serif designs.

Gill Sans Italic. The italic version of Gill Sans is also quite different from what one would expect to find in a sans serif design. An obliqued roman normally complements a roman sans serif. Gill Sans Italic is a strikingly different design from its upright counterpart. It is more condensed, slightly lighter, and contains several letters that are distinctly different designs from the roman versions. The lowercase *a*, for instance, is a single-storied character in the italic, and the roman is of the two-storied variety. The *f* descends below the baseline in the italic, but does not in the roman; and the italic *p* almost appears to be from a different typeface altogether—its main vertical stroke is lengthened and the stroke that defines the bowl is allowed to pass through it. In the capitals, the *C*, *G*, and *S* all have more exaggerated curves than would normally seem necessary.

Eric Gill's Big Family. As available from Monotype, the Gill Sans family is quite large, encompassing light, bold, and exceptionally heavy designs, condensed variations, an outline, two shadowed designs, something called *shadowline*, and a variety of other styles. In all, the basic Gill Sans letterforms sprawl across some thirty-six derivatives. Unfortunately, a small family is offered by most other type suppliers. Light, roman (or medium), bold, and extra bold versions in upright and italic mode are available from just about any major supplier. And some also offer condensed designs, an outline, and the very heavy display design—ultra bold (sometimes called Kayo). Even in abridged versions, however, the Gill Sans family is a powerful communications tool. It usually affords a sufficiently large and versatile group of variants to satisfy the needs of virtually any application.

In most sans serif typefaces, character counters all appear to be about the same size. There is an apparent regularity and order to the "doughnut holes." Gill Sans is different: The counters of the *a* and *e* are small; those in the *b*, *d*, *p*, and *q* are visually larger, and the *o* is larger still. This is not a design flaw—again, it is just because Gill Sans is based on the proportions of serif type. And, like most serif typestyles, those apparent design discrepancies blend into an even (and pleasant) typographic color when the letters are set together in words.

As with most typefaces, there are individual characters in Gill Sans that, although they serve no particular typographic service, help to distinguish it from other designs. Perhaps the most obvious are the lowercase *a*, *g*, and *t*. None of these look like the typical sans serif versions of those letters. Once again, the Gill Sans lineage of calligraphic letter-shapes has been made obvious. Other distinguishing lowercase letters are the *k*, because its diagonals meet at the stem (like Univers) rather than the lower diagonal connecting with the upper somewhere along its length, as in most sans serif designs, the *p* and the *q*, which have bowls that appear to attach at right angles (rather than a smooth curve) at the tops of the stems, and finally, the *f*, which has a top terminal that appears a little on the heavy side.

Although Eric Gill allowed his lowercase letters to have relatively proportional freedom, the caps in Gill Sans tend to be optically uniform in width: Every character appears to take an even amount of space.

BACKGROUND

The typographic communicator's palette was made richer through Eric Gill's work, yet he had few kind words for the art of typography. At different times, he is quoted as saying, "there are about as

Gill Sans

many different varieties of letters as there are fools"; "lettering has had its day"; and "the only way to reform modern lettering is to abolish it." Once, he even called master printers a "bunch of morons."

Because of his social and philosophical views, there can be little doubt that Gill considered type design as working for the enemy. Yet before he died in 1940, he created eleven typefaces, wrote influentially on typography, and with his son-in-law operated a commercial press.

Type's Dynamic Duo. How did Eric Gill's involvement with things typographic come about? Largely through the efforts of Stanley Morison, who was then the typographical advisor to Monotype. Morison believed his task as advisor was to change the "stiff, thin, regimental and savorless" typefaces then in use into designs that better reflected current typographic technology, thinking, and attitudes. After reviving several classical faces, such as Bembo and Fournier, he felt that a truly modern face (designed by a living artist) should be released, and he thought Gill was ideal for the job.

Morison felt that a serif typeface would be the best choice for a first design from Gill. In 1925, initial studies were begun for the typeface that was eventually to become Perpetua. Unfortunately, things did not go smoothly on Gill's first attempt at typeface design. Experiments, inconclusive trial cuttings, and innumerable revisions delayed the actual production of this face for several years. It was during this time that Morison persuaded Gill to work on a sans serif type.

Gill Sans was to be the British counterpart to Futura. Its purpose was to compete with the flood of sans serif designs that were being released by German foundries as a result of the overwhelming success of Futura.

Design Influences. Although the work was entirely his, there were two very strong influences on the sans serif typeface that Gill developed. The strongest influence was the work that Edward Johnston, Gill's mentor, did for the London Underground Railroad. The other influence

was Gill's own work—a set of alphabets he created for the British Army and Navy stores. Both influences were thus typefaces created primarily for signage purposes; and though there are obvious similarities between these and Gill's sans, his work differed in important, if subtle, ways from the predecessors.

When first shown at a trade conference in 1928, Gill Sans was greeted with something less than enthusiasm. In fact, the effort was generally panned. One critic even branded the design as "typographical Bolshevism" (a term that obviously was more damning in 1928 than it is today). A year later, when Gill Sans was released to the public, the cries had apparently subsided—or Gill was correct in his assessment of master printers—because the face became an almost instant success. Within a short time it became the most popular sans serif used in Britain and the United Kingdom. It was not until World War II, however, that Gill Sans was successfully exported outside the United Kingdom.

Currently, every manufacturer of graphic arts-quality composing equipment offers at least the basic Gill Sans family group. All are also of such a quality standard that one manufacturer's design need not be considered over others. It will probably be only a short time before this "most civilized of sans" becomes available on modest-resolution laser printers and desktop publishing systems.

CONSIDERATIONS FOR USE
Gill Sans was designed by someone who was a stone carver and calligrapher first and a type designer second. This does not mean that the face is not a good one; however, it tends to work and look best in situations similar to those for which calligraphy and lapidary inscriptions are best suited: in larger sizes and in modest-length documents. Text copy can be set in Gill Sans, but because it is a relatively small design to begin with, in sizes less than 10 point its readability suffers. It can be the perfect choice (especially the condensed designs) for such applications

abcdefgpqr
abcdefgpqr

Monotype introduced changes to Gill's calligraphy influenced type (top), e.g., eliminating slanting cut-offs on ascenders and descenders of the b, d, p, and q (bottom).

as directories, timetables, and reference material, where much information has to be set in a small space. At small sizes, Gill Sans is simply not especially enticing to the reader. If you are trying to coax potential readers into copy or provide them with many pages of comfortable reading, then use Gill Sans at a slightly larger size.

Gill Sans Light is an exceptionally beautiful—and delicate—typeface. The light weight of Gill can help produce some especially nice graphic communication, but it needs to be handled with a little care. Use it at larger sizes so that its full beauty can be appreciated and its faithful reproduction ensured. Avoid printing it in color, unless there is sufficient contrast with the background. And never (well, almost never) reverse Gill Sans Light out of a dark background.

Guaranteed Good Spacing. Gill Sans may appear to space just a little on the open side, but a second look reveals that it reads exceptionally well with its almost generous spacing. Tightening the spacing will quickly disrupt Gill's subtle harmony of positive and negative shapes; "hot" spots crop up, and all that is accomplished is a potential loss in readability. Gill Sans, however, is conducive to "constructive" typography and can be successfully letterspaced for heads and subheads.

The condensed variants of Gill Sans provide excellent alternatives to Helvetica or Univers where economy of space is a consideration. Just remember that Gill has character and will not fade into the background like Helvetica or Univers. For catalogs and parts lists that make a statement, Gill is the perfect choice.

Mixability. Gill Sans is a friendly face. It mixes well. It can be combined with members of its own family with the assurance of compatibility, and with the added benefit of a little extra variety not usually found by "mixing in family." Members of the Gill Sans family are obviously related, but sometimes do not appear to share the same set of parents. First, as the various versions become heavier, the contrasts in stroke weight become more pronounced (much more so than most sans serif designs). Second, individual character shapes and proportions do not always change consistently. Characters from one variant to another may relate in design but do not have the homogenized look found in many, more contemporary, sans serif families.

Gill also combines exceptionally well with types outside its immediate family. It is a natural contrast to serif typefaces, but with the added virtue that it also shares some underlying design similarities with many of these designs. Goudy Old Style, Baskerville, ITC Garamond, and a variety of other serif typestyles would all combine well with Gill Sans, producing design harmony, and perhaps this would also produce a subtle degree of graphic tension.

Most sans serif typefaces do not mix well with other sans serif styles. Their designs are too similar. Gill, because it does not look like most sans, is an exception. Gill Sans Bold or Kayo can easily provide heads or other display type to work with the light weights of Helvetica. Experiment a little with Gill Sans.

Line Space. Many sans serif typefaces, especially in the heavier weights, benefit from additional line space. Gill Sans, however, requires fewer spacing adjustments than most. Its small x-height and proportionally healthy ascenders and descenders produce a natural line space that improves reading ease. Even in its

heavier weights (excluding the Kayo), it can often be set *solid,* "with no leading," with no loss of clarity or attractiveness.

Line Length. Because it is a sans serif design, Gill Sans reads best when line lengths are not too long; most sans serifs operate best with an average of about nine words to a line. Gill, because of its distinct character shapes and built-in line space, can afford somewhat longer lines than most sans, but it is still not up to the holding power of a traditional serif typestyle. Because its proportions enable more words to be set in a given area than do most sans serif types, and because line lengths should be kept to no more than ten or eleven words, Gill Sans provides the opportunity to use white space to its maximum effectiveness. It is very easy to design light and airy or open and inviting typography when the services of Gill Sans are employed.

Where can Gill be put to use? Directory work, posters, short blocks of text, packaging, advertising of just about any sort—anywhere that great expanses of text copy are not required.

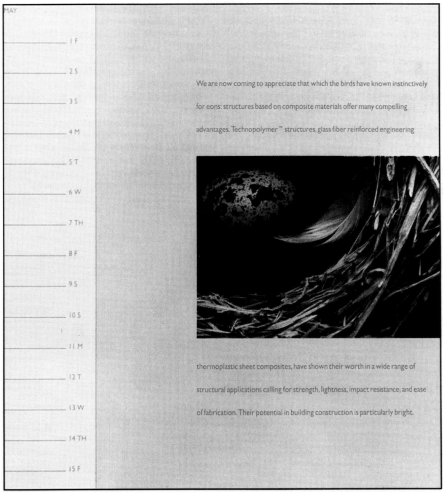

Designer Carol Bouchard used Gill Sans for a General Electric Plastics calendar for HBM/Creamer, Inc., because "it's clean, light and works well centered or ragged, anywhere on the page."

Goudy Old Style

ABCDEFGHIJKLMNOPQRSTUVWXYZ
abcdefghijklmnopqrstuvwxyz
1234567890
$)] - ; / — , . ! ([& - : / ? , . ¢ ¿ ¡ ß £ / — „ ·

ABCDEFGHIJKLMNOPQRSTUVWXYZ
abcdefghijklmnopqrstuvwxyz
1234567890
$)] - ; / — , . ! ([& - : / ? , . ¢ ¿ ¡ ß £ / — „ ·

Goudy Old Style

Goudy Old Style Italic

Goudy Bold

Goudy Bold Italic

Goudy Extra Bold

Goudy Heavyface

Goudy Heavyface Italic

Goudy Heavyface Condensed

Goudy Handtooled

Goudy Old Style was Frederic Goudy's first type design for ATF. He went on to design many more faces for this and other foundries, but none of them have proved to be quite as popular as this classic design.

ATTRIBUTES

Goudy Old Style, as many of Goudy's faces, is based on the early work of Italian type designers. The diagonal stress of the character strokes is the most obvious trait of these early Venetian Old Style type designs. In Goudy Old Style this stress in the curves of characters like the *b, c, d,* and *p* is quite marked. The descenders in Goudy Old Style are short in comparison with other classic Old Style faces, and Frederic Goudy felt that this was a flaw in his design. He originally drew them longer, but the technical requirements of metal type forced them to be shortened to maintain a consistent baseline with other typefaces offered by ATF. This trait has no ill effects on typeface readability, but it does make what would normally be an elegant design appear just a little chunky.

The x-height of Goudy Old Style is generous but not excessive, and character proportions are on the expanded side. This means that the face, not ideally suited to applications where space is at a premium, will maintain high levels of character legibility at small sizes. Complementing these expansive character proportions are the high, rounded arches in characters like the *h* and *n*.

When a Lighter Touch Is Needed. Goudy Old Style is no heavyweight. It is a light, almost delicate design. Although it can impart a feeling of elegance or sophistication to an application (in spite of its smallish descenders), Goudy Old Style is not the face to choose when reading conditions are less than optimum. Goudy Old Style can be the perfect type for an annual report, business proposal, or

quality brochure; but not for newsletters or directories.

Many feel that Goudy Old Style Italic is Goudy's best italic design. In it he kept the degree of slant to a minimum and character proportions condensed. In later designs Goudy allowed his italics to become more slanted with wider traits, which detracted from their elegance and charm. Although italics are generally not the best communications tools, Goudy Old Style Italic has been recommended by many typographic experts as an excellent choice for display applications and short blocks of text copy.

There are many other distinguishing characteristics of the Goudy Old Style family: the variations and slight curvature of the serifs; the large, round capital letters such as the *O, U, C,* and *G*; the diamond-shaped dots used for punctuation marks and for the lowercase *i* and *j*; and the delicate curved strokes found in many letters, such as the bottom arm of the capital *E* and *L* and the lower diagonal of the lowercase *k*.

BACKGROUND

Frederic Goudy was probably one of the most prolific text typeface designers. Even today, most type specimen books are filled with Goudy designs. They are easy to spot because most are named after him.

Goudy began work on Goudy Old Style in 1912 when he received a commission to design a new typeface for a book on Abraham Lincoln. He labored over the face for several months and even got to the stage where type was cast and sample pages were set. But when the sponsor of the book died and money for the venture ceased to come in, Goudy had to turn to other projects.

British Interest in an American Face. After it sat on the shelf for several months, Goudy decided to revive the design and market it himself as Goudy Old Style. A

large British typefoundry saw the design and inquired whether they could license the rights to it and issue the face as theirs. Goudy agreed, but with the explicit stipulation that the foundry produce his design with no modifications or changes. A deal was struck and production began. When Goudy saw the completed product, however, he learned that sometimes "front-office" promises are not honored by those responsible for carrying them out. Indeed, many changes were made to his original design.

Goudy traveled to the foundry in an attempt to save what he felt was the better design. Unfortunately the "die had been cast," and as far as the foundry was concerned, no changes were possible. The managers of the foundry were apologetic, and they even showed great enthusiasm for the additional design proposals Goudy had brought with him, yet no additional work on Goudy Old Style would be possible, and no further typefaces from the designer could be put into their production schedule.

Goudy's traveling companion on this journey, Clarence Marder, was impressed by the sincerity of the foundry's regrets—and even more impressed with their enthusiasm for Goudy's design proposals. This was fortunate for Goudy, because Marder was also in the type business. He was associated with one of the more important foundries of ATF.

After their return from England, Marder spoke with the president of ATF and suggested that he invite Goudy to the corporate offices in New Jersey to discuss a possible business arrangement. The invitation was sent, and Goudy accepted. The resulting meeting was quite short; after pleasantries were exchanged, ATF's chief executive officer asked Goudy if he would consider creating a face for the ATF type library. Goudy agreed, but again with the explicit stipulation that no changes or modifications be performed on his original work. Marder agreed and arrangements were made.

Goudy Old Style

AREAS OF ACTIVITY

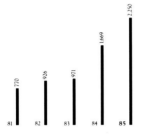

**Average Daily Net Production
Crude Oil and Condensate**
Barrels per day

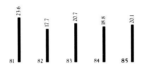

**Average Daily Net Production
Natural Gas**
MMCF per day

Mississippi:

The company's easternmost area of significant production is the Diamond Field of Wayne County, Mississippi. In December 1983 Cenergy purchased a 100 percent working interest in seven Diamond Field wells, which collectively were producing approximately 80 barrels of oil per day from the Glen Rose, Hosston and Cotton Valley formations. Through the close of fiscal 1985, the company had drilled three new development wells in the field and had completed several workovers and recompletions, one of which resulted in a new pool discovery, the Lower Hosston Pool. Production at year end had been raised to more than 1,000 barrels per day.

Northwest of the Diamond Field, in Rankin County, Mississippi, is the Thomasville Field, where Cenergy has an average 25 percent working interest in four unregulated, deep sour gas wells producing from the Smackover formation. In addition, the company has a one-quarter interest in a gas processing and sulphur recovery plant at the field. The company began its Thomasville activities in 1977 with the drilling of the first of the wells, and the processing plant became operational allowing gas production to start up during the third quarter of fiscal 1981. For fiscal 1985, the Thomasville Field represented about 27 percent of Cenergy's gas revenues and 16 percent of total gas volumes produced.

Louisiana:

In 1979 Cenergy purchased an approximate 10 percent position in the eastern part of the Moore-Sams Field in Pointe Coupee Parish, Louisiana. A discovery well was completed as a gas producer in January 1980, and went on production in July 1981. Cenergy has participated in the drilling of 16 Moore-Sams wells, of which 12 have been productive from the Lower Tuscaloosa sands between 18,000 and 20,000 feet. Cenergy's portion of the curtailed production averaged 1,100 MCF of gas per day during fiscal 1985, representing about 10 percent of the company's gas revenues and five percent of total gas produced.

To the west, in Acadia Parish, Cenergy has a 15 percent interest in the MM Sand Unit of the East Richie Field, where 26 wells produce at a depth of about 3,800 feet, and interests in eight additional field wells outside the unit. The company, which began operations in this field in 1974, had net production of approximately 248 barrels of oil per day from the field during fiscal 1985.

In 1983 Cenergy discovered the Southeast Saturday Island Field in Plaquemines Parish. The field, operated by Cenergy, is located in shallow water in Barataria Bay and went on production in January 1984. Its three wells, two of which are dually completed, produce from Miocene sands between 10,400 and 12,450 feet.

Joe Rattan and Woody Pirtle of Pirtle Design, Dallas, chose Goudy Old Style for their design of Cenergy's 1985 annual report because of its classic look and readable numbers.

Goudy says that the inspiration for the design came from a few letters copied from the bottom of a portrait painted by Hans Holbein. The letters were only in capital form, so Goudy set for himself the difficult task of completing not only the alphabet as it had been started, but also creating a set of lowercase characters in harmony with the capitals. Normally, alphabets are conceived and drawn the other way around, with the lowercase drawn first.

Goudy did have, as he put it, some "troubles" with the transfer of his drawings into typefaces. It seems that the design staff at ATF had the same difficulty as the British foundry in living up to the promise of "hands off" concerning Goudy's original work. Once again Goudy was forced to remind them of their commitment. This time he was more successful in reaching his goals. The president of ATF gave orders that no changes should be made to Goudy's work unless he agreed to them, and that the already changed characters should be replaced with ones that followed Goudy's drawings exactly. The orders were carried out to the letter, and the only modification to Goudy's drawings was the shortening of the descenders, which, of course, Goudy agreed to. What did concern him, however, was that ATF went on to design Goudy Bold, Goudy Bold Italic, Goudy Extra Bold, Goudy Extra Bold Italic, and Goudy Title without his aid or approval.

The completed family of roman and italic was released by ATF in 1915 as Goudy Old Style. The previous British Goudy Old Style had been released under the name Ratdolt—yet another change that Goudy did not agree with. This change, however, gave Goudy and ATF the opportunity to use the name that Goudy approved of.

CONSIDERATIONS FOR USE

Few conditions are outside Goudy Old Style's range. It has been used successfully in just about every typographic application. While it does not include all the design traits of a true legibility design, Goudy Old Style does maintain high levels of legibility and is conducive to the requirements of readable typography. The generous x-height, full counters, moderate contrast in stroke variance, and relatively sturdy serifs add up to a design that is ideally suited to lengthy text composition. Advertising copy, annual reports, and even complete magazines have been set in Goudy Old Style.

Because it is a rather light face, Goudy Old Style will not reverse as well as some other faces; for the same reason, care should be taken when using it to print on rough or textured paper stock. Aside from this, Goudy Old Style will reproduce well on a wide range of papers, even on coated stocks where the thicks and thins of some typefaces create the dazzling effect, which quickly tires the reader's eyes.

Goudy Old Style has few limitations in its size range. It can be used with success down to 7 or 8 point, and it looks well in large display sizes. Many typefaces that work well at text sizes do not make a comfortable transition to display work and vice versa. Goudy Old Style can create beautiful headlines and be used to set small captions or footnotes.

Because it is such a popular typeface, and perhaps because it is in the public domain and has such a clear lineage, Goudy Old Style is available as a consistently high quality rendering from virtually every graphic-arts supplier. There is little risk in specifying this typestyle.

One problem with this family is its size. The full family can be counted on two fingers. There are bold and bold italic versions in other Goudy designs—but not here. This limits its use in many normal text-setting environments. When emphasis is required, a face from a different family must be pressed into service. As long as this circumstance exists, it might make sense to take advantage of it and use a different design to add emphasis or impact. Try Helvetica Bold Condensed or Glypha 65 as a companion to Goudy Old Style: The results can be dynamic and even provocative.

There are some condensed variants of Goudy Old Style offered by a few suppliers, but these are electronically extrapolated designs, and they do not have the grace or refinement of the Goudy originals. Like most electronically generated italics, they should be avoided.

Although there is no such thing as an evocative typeface that unfailingly inspires consistent feelings or emotions, Goudy Old Style seems to bring a quality of elegance to any piece in which it is used. It is an exceptionally beautiful design; perhaps this beauty transcends the normal levels of influence a typeface can have on the finished piece. It is hard to go wrong with Goudy Old Style.

Helvetica

ABCDEFGHIJKLMNOPQRSTUVWXYZ
abcdefghijklmnopqrstuvwxyz
1234567890
$)] - ; / — , . ! ([& - : / ? , . ¢ ¿ ¡ ß £ / — „ ·

ABCDEFGHIJKLMNOPQRSTUVWXYZ
abcdefghijklmnopqrstuvwxyz
1234567890
$)] - ; / — , . ! ([& - : / ? , . ¢ ¿ ¡ ß £ / — „ ·

Helvetica Thin
Helvetica Thin Italic
Helvetica Light
Helvetica Light Italic
Helvetica
Helvetica Italic
Helvetica Bold
Helvetica Bold Italic
Helvetica Heavy
Helvetica Heavy Italic
Helvetica Black
Helvetica Black Italic

This popular sans serif typeface has such a clean look that it can be used for every imaginable typesetting situation.

ATTRIBUTES

Sans serif types are generally subclassified into three groups: geometric, calligraphic, and nineteenth-century grotesques. Faces like Futura and ITC Avant Garde Gothic fall into the first category, the second embraces designs like Optima and Gill Sans, and the last is home for faces like Univers, ITC Franklin Gothic, and Helvetica.

One of the difficulties with nineteenth-century grotesques is that they tend to look alike: The typographic neophyte (and often those who have worked with type for a long time) can have difficulty distinguishing one from another. There are, however, subtle differences between these designs, and it is these nuances that can make one or another better suited to a particular application.

Of all nineteenth-century grotesques, Helvetica has some of the least apparent changes in weight stress. Although it is not as monotone in weight as its geometric cousins, it is, to the casual observer, constructed of optically similar stroke weights. This trait can make Helvetica a little difficult to read in some circumstances. Large blocks of text copy set in a relatively monoweight typestyle have a tendency to tire the reader and slow down the reading process. The eye apparently needs a little sparkle and vibrancy to hold its interest in text copy.

The capital letters in all nineteenth-century grotesques are virtual copies of each other. You could probably substitute the caps from one face into another without anyone noticing. The only distinguishing feature about Helvetica's capitals is that they are slightly more expanded than those found in faces like Folio or Univers.

Lowercase Identifiers. Although there are subtle differences, the lowercase of ITC Franklin Gothic or Univers or Helvetica share designs that are almost as close to one another as their capital counterparts. The two-storied *a* is, however, an easy identifier for Helvetica. The stem curves to the right at the baseline, and the bowl has a gentle curve where it meets the stem. Other lowercase letters that help identify the design are the somewhat narrow *t* and *f* and the slightly square looking *s*. In addition, the numeral *1* in Helvetica has a bracketed top serif.

More than any other single design, Helvetica is responsible for ushering in the age of increased x-heights. Similar styles like Standard, Folio, Venus, and even the ATF version of Franklin Gothic have shorter lowercase letters. When Helvetica was released in 1957, it was one of the first typestyles with enlarged character proportions. As Helvetica grew in popularity, so did the large x-heights for new typefaces.

BACKGROUND

Helvetica is probably read by more people in a wider variety of printed media than any other single type design. The typestyle is available from virtually all suppliers of graphic-arts typefonts and from any type house or service bureau. Because of its popularity, most manufacturers are obligated to supply high-caliber versions of this face to their customers. As a result, the typestyle comes the closest to being a consistent design from all suppliers.

Helvetica's lineage can be traced back to the late 1800s, to a typeface called Akzidenz Grotesk first released by the Berthold foundry. In the mid-1950s, Edouard Hoffman at the Haas Typefoundry in Switzerland felt that even though there had been numerous designs, and redesigns, based on the Akzidenz Grotesk style, a new version was in order.

Hoffman approached Max Miedinger and they worked out the new design. Hoffman provided the concept while Miedinger did the drawing. They worked well together, producing many trial sketches and test fonts prior to settling on the final design. In 1957 the result of their collaboration was released as New Haas Grotesk.

New Foundry, New Name. In 1961, the parent company of Haas in Frankfurt, Stempel, decided to offer the design to their customers in Germany. They made some changes to the proportions of the face to enable its output on linecasting equipment. Stempel felt that they would be unable to market a new face under another foundry's name (even if they owned that foundry) and looked for a name that would embody the spirit and heritage of the face. They settled on Helvetica. Hoffman was shocked, declaring that Helvetica too closely resembled the name of Switzerland (Helvetia) and was unsuitable for a typeface. Stempel used it anyway, and several months later Haas was forced to adopt it for themselves.

In 1964, Stempel's parent company, Mergenthaler Linotype, after watching the steady sales growth of the design, adapted Helvetica for their equipment. Linotype, which was then an American company, fortunately did not see the same need as Stempel to change the typeface's name. If they did, we could be specifying "Dutchland," or something like it, today.

Originally, only roman designs of Helvetica were released by Haas; it took four years before the first italics were offered.

New designs and weights were created over the years to complement the initial release, so that today the Helvetica type family has over twenty different faces. In addition to roman, medium, and boldface, the family also includes thin, light, heavy, black, extra black condensed, bold outline, and contour, among others. Unfortunately, these were designed by several designers and not under a well-defined development program. The result is a patchwork type family. Though the basic design traits are inherent in every design, the full Helvetica family does not have the design unity and order that can be found in faces like Univers.

Helvetica

1940s, will be utterly synthesized into the convolution of mountain ranges taking on the reverberating forms of the inner ear alluded to in *Whispering*, the flat mountain ranges represented in discrete patches of green, gray, and white before which the bone shapes and implements (which would become the principal elements of the "Dunstlöcher" series begun in late 1935) are statically displayed. In other words two pictures painted at the same time exchange technique and thematics, the flat natural literalness of the one acquiring the dynamic movement of the other, the inner ear becoming the upheaving mountain, an image of sound becoming the means of visualizing nature's transformations. The other two paintings, *Wind* 1934/2,[52] and *Segelplastik* (*Sail Sculpture* 1934/13), anticipate the weather signal paintings that predominate in the "Signs and Signals" series begun in 1939 and continued throughout the early 1940s.

The "Dunstlöcher" Paintings: Soft Form Paintings (1935-1937)

Beginning in the early 1950s, Bayer got into the habit of developing a brief statement to set forth the historical suggestion, autobiographic occasion, or aesthetic attitude implicit in each series of paintings upon which he was engaged. Such brief statements, never more than 750 words, served to recollect and interpret paintings done several decades earlier, but as the years have passed, they have enabled him as well to define the underlying intention of each group of paintings as a way of completing a series, and to develop a springboard for a series about to be inaugurated. Bayer thinks in an extremely orderly manner, his mind, like his desk, tidy, lineated, clean; and yet, despite such apparent fastidiousness, he is not always able to find what he's looking for, which is as healthy in painting as it is disconcerting in desk management. It is no wonder that the modest statement Bayer wrote in 1970 to recollect his thinking about the first coherent group of paintings that he annotated—the "Dunstlöcher" images of 1935-1937—as clearly as it elucidates their origin, remains enigmatic in explanation of the paintings themselves:

my fascination with and admiration for the old peasant houses dates back to my wandervogel days (1916-1919), when I hiked through the austrian countryside. of special interest to me were the barns and stables into which were cut windows of various and ornamental shapes, which are probably of baroque origin. these "windows" serve as vents for the hay stored in the barns and are called "dunstlöcher" (vapor or haze holes). against those barn walls, all sorts of implements for the peasant to use in agriculture were leaned or hung on hooks—shovels, rakes, harrows, threshing clubs, ladders, hook, poles to hang the hay to dry in the fields, ropes, etc.

it was later, during the thirties, that I remembered these barns and stables and painted a series of "dunstlöcher" paintings. their poetic and surreal conception is perhaps best represented by *barn windows*, (1926/11) painted in oil. I can understand why these paintings have less meaning for those who do not know the archaic nature of this subject, which is usually judged to have only sculptural interest. a three dimensional character is, of course, indigenous to these paintings, as my several attempts to make

Shadow over Cone 1934/3, gouache, 14 x 11″.
Collection Joella Bayer.

Helvetica was selected by the late Bauhaus artist Herbert Bayer for all of the copy in his biography, *Herbert Bayer*, by Arthur A. Cohen (MIT Press). In deference to Bayer's commitment to using only the lowercase alphabet, his direct quotations appeared in this way throughout the text, as in the last two paragraphs of the page shown here.

To further complicate matters, designs created for machine composition were different in proportion, and in many cases weight range, from their hand-set counterparts. And when phototypesetting equipment came along, yet another, slightly different, version of the basic design was created. Even Linotype, in an ad for Helvetica in the 1970s, stated, "Since the series was not planned as a whole conception, as was the case with Univers, the series is not as uniform as Univers. . . . Where a broad range of weights, widths, and italics are required in a single job, Univers is the logical device."

CONSIDERATIONS FOR USE

If you were to characterize Helvetica's typestyle in one word, that word would be *universal*. It has been used for every typesetting application imaginable. And it is probably suitable for each and every one of those applications. Many designers claim that they could do all their work with just Helvetica and one other typestyle. Helvetica is an easy face to use well. Poor reading conditions, less-than-ideal paper stock, and difficult design applications are all within its realm. Hel-vetica is not only versatile, it is also forgiving. Pushed to extremes, it still rewards the graphic communicator with predictable results. Because of this predictability factor, Helvetica usually can be an excellent choice for rush jobs. It is available everywhere, in every imaginable form, and is almost always in an acceptable—if not high quality—form.

Because it is a sans serif with a large x-height and strong vertical stress, try to maintain close, even word spacing for maximum readability. To further aid the reader, letterspacing can be a little tighter than supplied in stock from many vendors, although if you do opt for "minus letterspacing" be sure that the color of the resulting copy is even, with no dark spots where letters come too close or touch. Line length should be limited to about nine or ten words. Because Helvetica lacks the benefit of typographic baseline retainers (serifs), long lines are not as easily or efficiently read as they would be with Times Roman or Century Schoolbook.

Helvetica can be combined with just about any other typestyle—except for its close, nineteenth-century grotesque cousins. It can be mixed with some of the other sans serifs, but this is pretty risky business, even for the "universal" Helvetica. Most sans serifs do not combine well with each other because their design traits, proportions, and stroke characteristics are too similar to contrast well, and just dissimilar enough (unless they are from the same family) not to complement. The result of mixing sans serif designs from different families is almost always less than ideal. Although as the Linotype ad stated that it is not as good as Univers for complicated "in-family" work, Helvetica is still a very good choice for those applications that call for numerous typeface changes. The basic face gives unity and consistency to a piece, while the diverse range of weights and variants provide a rich typographic palette. Complicated textbooks, annual reports, training manuals, and price lists are naturals for Helvetica.

Use the condensed design where space is at a premium. Use the bold weights for strong, forceful headlines, and medium and light weights for practically any application you want. Aside from these tips, you should have no trouble using Helvetica for any project you have in mind.

ITC Korinna

ABCDEFGHIJKLMNOPQRSTUVWXYZ
abcdefghijklmnopqrstuvwxyz
1234567890
$)] - ; / — , . ! ([& - : / ? , . ¢ ¿ ¡ ß £ / — „ ·

ABCDEFGHIJKLMNOPQRSTUVWXYZ
abcdefghijklmnopqrstuvwxyz
1234567890
$)] - ; / — , . ! ([& - : / ? , . ¢ ¿ ¡ ß £ / — „ ·

ITC Korinna

ITC Korinna Kursiv

ITC Korinna Bold

ITC Korinna Bold Kursiv

ITC Korinna Extra Bold

ITC Korinna Extra Bold Kursiv

ITC Korinna Heavy

ITC Korinna Heavy Kursiv

ITC Korinna Bold Outline

Generally, the most versatile typefaces are those that lack a distinct personality. Times Roman is a perfect example: It can be used for virtually any typographic application; and though it is beautiful, it is a design distinctly lacking in personality. Then there is ITC Korinna, which somehow manages to combine the qualities of versatility and distinction.

ATTRIBUTES

ITC Korinna is a relatively monotone design with a large x-height, small serifs—and an odd *g*. Unfortunately, although accurate, this description of the typeface does not come close to telling the complete ITC Korinna story. This is also a face with style and verve, one with a long and complex background, and one that defies simple pigeonholing.

ITC Korinna is a typeface caught between two worlds: the sensual, provocative world of the art nouveau movement and the systematic, rational world of most German typeface designs. The result is a typographic workhorse—but one with a fair amount of distinction and spirit—sort of a Volkswagen with a Porsche engine.

Although often called a *monoweight* design, ITC Korinna does have subtle contrast in character stroke weight. This good (maybe even necessary) design trait ensures reader involvement and interest. Strict monoweight designs such as Futura, Italia, or City have a tendency to demotivate readers. ITC Korinna is never going to be confused with Bodoni or ITC Modern No. 216, but it has more than enough character stroke contrast to maintain active reader participation. ITC Korinna is, however, a borderline case. If lengthy text copy is set with little regard for other typographic considerations, the stroke weight contrast of ITC Korinna will not save the day. Its contrast ratio should be considered a benefit, not a dominant asset.

ITC Korinna is slightly expanded. It is what one would have described, several years ago, as a typeface with a "wide set." "Way back when" (before laser printers, digital fonts, and electronic italicizing), designers had used a basic building block with which to develop new typefaces. This was the em square: a unit equal to the point size of the type squared. (A 10-point em square would be 10 points high by 10 points wide.) Obviously, the em square determined the height of type, and to a large extent, it also determined the width. To establish intercharacter spacing, the horizontal of the em square was divided into eighteen spaces. Each letter was then designed to fit within and have lateral spacing defined by a given number of those eighteen units. This process worked for typefaces of normal proportions, but those that were narrower or wider than normal were limited in spacing range by the standard system. For cases such as this, the hardware engineers devised a method to fool the typesetting equipment. Through a series of mechanical adjustments, usually performed by the equipment operator, the eighteen units could be condensed down to something less than the point size (narrow set) or stretched out to something wider than normal (wide set). ITC Korinna would have been designed to something slightly wider than a "normal" set.

New Member of the Legibility Family. Although ITC Korinna is probably never going to be mistaken for Century Schoolbook, Excelsior, or the other paragons of legibility, it does maintain remarkable levels of typographic clarity. Oddly enough, this is to some extent due to the design's art nouveau heritage. ITC Korinna has some very distinctive character shapes, which help to differentiate what could in many cases almost be considered similar letters; for example, a single-storied *g* normally is not as legible as the more common loop and bowl version found in Times Roman or Baskerville. But ITC Korinna has the very distinctive "Benguiat hook" to the *g*'s descending stroke that helps to define the character.

Other traits that help to ensure ITC Korinna's high legibility factors are its relatively large x-height, strong (but not dominant) serifs, and a character stroke weight that is sturdy while benefiting from a certain amount of contrast.

Included among the characters that help to distinguish ITC Korinna from other designs are the capital *C* and *G*, which have an unusually curved bowl. In addition, the *G* has a remarkably tall vertical stroke. The cap *M* is splayed, with middle strokes descending only part of the way to the baseline. The capital *N* has an abbreviated diagonal, and the cap *U* has a distinctive bow to its first stroke. In the lowercase, the *b, c, g, p,* and *q* all share the same sensual bowl found in the capital letters.

Fancy Versus Not So Fancy. ITC Korinna's fancy alternative design is a face called Korinna Kursiv. This is an original work by Benguiat that replaces the simpler, less effective, obliqued roman of the Berthold version. True to form, Benguiat has created a typeface design that has something special about it. Most italic types are more condensed than their roman counterparts and are, usually, optically lighter in weight. Not so with ITC Korinna Kursiv. It has the same robust proportions and strength of line as its upright relative. Although some of the delicacy and grace normally found in italic designs may be missing in this style, it more than makes up for these possible shortcomings in its ability to triumph over poor printing and reading conditions. ITC Korinna Kursiv is italic that your audience can read.

BACKGROUND

For most typefaces, one introduction is enough. Sometimes, as with revival designs, it takes two. Korinna needed three. The first was in 1904 during the height of the German Jugendstil (art nouveau) movement. Then, some time later, the Korinna design showed up in the Intertype (an American company) specimen book as a new introduction for their slug casting machines. At this point, the pictures in the Korinna family album get a little fuzzy. Although the Intertype version is clearly called Korinna, with no similarity implied, the design was modified from the Berthold master. Gone are many of the blatant art nouveau overtones, character proportions have been expanded, and even the x-height was enlarged slightly. Actually, the current Korinna owes more of its design to the Intertype font than it does to the German original.

Berthold's Korinna enjoyed only modest popularity in Europe. The Intertype transplant was an even less successful business venture. Within a relatively short time, the Korinna design ceased to be offered as a vital part of anybody's product line; it became virtually extinct.

Third Time's the Charm. In 1973, Korinna had its third release; this time the results were much more positive. As a result of a license agreement with Berthold, ITC was able to commission Benguiat and Victor Caruso to revive the original Korinna design. Their directive was simple: Keep the style and personality of the German design, but make it more applicable to current tastes and technology. The result is ITC Korinna, a family of four weights with corresponding italics.

Even the ITC version, with all the backing of ITC's creative marketing support, was a rather slow starter. It was not immediately picked up by all of the company's subscribers, and it saw relatively little use by graphic communicators the first year or two of its availability. As Aaron Burns, ITC's founder, once said, "Some typefaces, like fine wine, must age before they are ready." Slowly, designers began to use the family—with positive results. As a consequence, more designers asked for ITC Korinna, and more ITC subscribers included the family as part of their type offering. Finally, the seventy-five-year-old German transplant found a permanent home. Today, over

Because ITC Korinna is "distinctive yet readable," says Eileen Adler, graphic-services manager for Budget Rent A Car, it is used in many of their ads.

fourteen years after its introduction, ITC Korinna is consistently one of ITC's ten best-selling typefaces.

CONSIDERATIONS FOR USE

ITC Korinna has often been called a workhorse typeface. Sometimes it is called a "workhorse with distinction," sometimes a "designer's workhorse." Various adjectives are linked with it, but the respected draft animal is almost always part of the description. What typophiles are trying to tell us by this comparison is that we can pick virtually any typographic application, set it in ITC Korinna, and be assured of good, solid service. Magazines, books, newsletters, advertisements, brochures, even movie titles, have been successfully—and beautifully—set in ITC Korinna.

Workhorses are not considered to be especially elegant or sophisticated animals. They are big, robust creatures that can do a variety of tasks with relatively little fuss. So it is with ITC Korinna. This sturdy typeface can work under a variety of typographic conditions with predictably successful results.

About the only thing ITC Korinna does not do particularly well is save space. The large x-height of ITC Korinna and ample set-width do not make the design especially well suited to the setting of directories, parts lists, time tables, and similar documents.

Two Faces in One. ITC Korinna performs exceptionally well as a text face. At 10 and 12 point, it becomes a straightforward, no-nonsense communications tool. Then, as its size is increased, the design begins to unveil its distinctive characteristics. The end result is that ITC Korinna can be used for both text and display composition in the same job and (almost) appear to be different faces.

Like its animal counterpart, ITC Korinna should not be corralled in small spaces. It needs room to breathe naturally and feel comfortable. First, since this is not a featherweight design, even its lightest version has ample strength to withstand the least favorable typographic conditions. This means that if it is spaced too tightly, either in letterspacing or line spacing values, it will produce a rather heavy looking page—not the best way to attract and hold readers. In addition, if set with negative letterspacing, the close-fitting characters will not blend well with the naturally open counters. Here the result will be even worse: uneven typographic color.

This is no wallflower. ITC Korinna is a face that is easily seen. It does not fade into the background, creating a soft, watercolor-gray page. This is a design that, because of its proportions and weight, stands out. The concern is that if ITC Korinna is set too tight in text composition, if its line space values are zero or less, or if it is allowed to fill long, unbroken columns, the end result can be heavy, uninviting, and difficult to read.

The good news is that as its point size is increased, ITC Korinna rewards the graphic communicator with additional latitude in spacing—and a marked ability to attract attention. It is in display applications that ITC Korinna makes best use of its art nouveau heritage. At anything above 18 point, its vigorous design traits begin to make themselves known and do a surprisingly effective job of catching the reader's eye. An added benefit is that the short serifs invite relatively snug letterspacing.

Lots of Color. Type works best when it is printed in dark ink on a light background. A few faces can put up with being reversed out of a dark background, and fewer still can stand being printed in a wide spectrum of colors. ITC Korinna is pretty much "bulletproof" when it comes to color printing. It reverses with ease—and with virtually no drop in communications power. It shines in strong colors and performs as well as can be expected of any type in light or soft colors.

Mixability. ITC Korinna is an exceptionally gregarious design. It likes to mix with other typestyles—all kinds of typestyles. The moderate weight stress and short, thick serifs of this design contrast beautifully with Modern and Old Style designs alike. Try combining ITC Korinna with Bodoni or Goudy Old Style. ITC Korinna can also be mixed with virtually any gothic—from Frutiger to Futura. ITC Korinna Extra Bold would dramatically contrast with text copy set in ITC Goudy Sans Book or Frutiger 45. Or consider contrasting the delicate elegance of Optima with the strength and forcefulness of ITC Korinna Heavy. ITC Korinna can be mixed with Meridian, Caledonia, or even Gill Sans; the combinations are almost limitless.

Of course, no one gets along with everybody. ITC Korinna draws the line at other open, heavy serif designs. Even though they are from a common design source, ITC Korinna and ITC Bookman probably are going to be rather difficult to mix successfully. Also, faces like Melior and Rockwell should probably not be combined with ITC Korinna.

Availability. ITC Korinna is available in four weights: Regular, Bold, Extra Bold, and Heavy. Each has a Kursiv counterpart, and most even have a few alternate characters for display setting. Small caps are not available, but do not ask your typographer to electronically generate the small caps. The end result will look out of place in any copy.

Finally, you will not have any trouble ordering ITC Korinna. Every manufacturer of graphic arts typesetting equipment offers it; it can be found on dry transfer sheets and even on low resolution printers.

Typophiles tend to be very particular folks, not generally welcoming funny-looking or odd characters into their midst. It took three tries, and many years, but now ITC Korinna is firmly established as a typophile's friend—funny looking g's and all.

Memphis

ABCDEFGHIJKLMNOPQRSTUVWXYZ
abcdefghijklmnopqrstuvwxyz
1234567890
$)] - ; / — , . ! ([& - : / ? , . ¢ ¿ ¡ ß £ / — „ ·

ABCDEFGHIJKLMNOPQRSTUVWXYZ
abcdefghijklmnopqrstuvwxyz
1234567890
$)] - ; / — , . ! ([& - : / ? , . ¢ ¿ ¡ ß £ / — „

Memphis Light
Memphis Light Italic
Memphis Medium
Memphis Medium Italic
Memphis Bold
Memphis Bold Italic
Memphis Extra Bold

Many typefaces lead dual lives in design usage. Times Roman was designed for text composition but is equally at home in display headlines. The same holds true for Helvetica, ITC Garamond, Century Old Style, and a variety of other designs.

Usually this duality is confined to typefaces that are originally drawn as text designs; rarely does one with display origins become an acceptable text face, but it does happen.

Egyptians, or square serif typefaces, are such an exception. This style of type was first developed to satisfy the need for heavy, attention-getting alphabets in the fledgling years of the advertising industry. They were created to be display types of the highest order. Today they are used for a variety of text as well as display applications. One important square serif is Memphis.

ATTRIBUTES

Memphis is marked by square, or flat and blunt, serifs. They are usually heavy, quite prominent, and, as a rule, as thick as the strokes they terminate. These serifs are almost never bracketed, and when they are, the typestyle is normally classified as a Clarendon rather than as a square serif.

Most of the more popular designs tend to appear, like sans serifs, monoweight—having character strokes that are optically the same. This comparison to sans serif design traits applies to other aspects of the design also. In fact, several of the most popular styles are based on sans serif typefaces. Memphis, the first of the popular twentieth-century square serifs, has been called "Futura with serifs." ITC Lubalin Graph was developed with the same proportions and design characteristics as ITC Avant Garde Gothic, and Glypha, by Adrian Frutiger, is based on his earlier design Univers.

Square serif typestyles have a tendency toward large x-heights and simple character shapes. Both these attributes provide for high levels of typeface legibility.

BACKGROUND

Square serif typestyles were first introduced in 1815, about the same time as sans serif styles. Interestingly, both originated in England and were first made available as caps-only designs. It was perhaps even more coincidental that William Caslon IV, who produced the first sans serif, called this design Egyptian, the term by which most square serif styles are also known today.

By 1825, square serif typefaces were designed as full fonts with lowercase characters, and, by 1850, they were available as large families containing several weights and design variants.

These early square-serif typefaces represented one of the first examples of what is now commonplace in the design and marketing of typefaces—creating a typestyle to meet the requirements of a specific application or set of circumstances. In the early part of the nineteenth century, the Industrial Revolution was just beginning to pick up steam. It was already apparent, however, that an important byproduct of the Industrial Revolution was advertising.

Prior to advertising, typefaces were primarily designed for books and continuous reading. These designs, though excellent for use in text composition, were unsuitable for attracting attention or delivering a quick message at large sizes. The first square serif designs were created for the sole purpose of enhancing advertising typography. They could claim the title of the first true display typefaces.

The popularity of these square serif types lasted until the first part of the twentieth century, when their use declined rapidly. This disuse continued for almost thirty years until square serif typefaces were revived as text designs by several German typefounders. (Actually, one of the first revivals was an American design, released by ATF, but it was not used much until after the German designs were imported into the United States.)

Memphis, from the Stempel foundry in Germany, is credited with starting the square serif revival. It was released in 1929, but was soon followed by Beton from the Bauer foundry, City from Berthold, and Luxor from Ludwig and Mayer—all German companies. Other European foundries followed suit; Nilo and Egizio were released in Italy, and Rockwell and Scarab were issued in Britain.

Many of these designs were imported to the United States, where most became popular also. As a counter to this influx of European types, ATF rereleased, in 1931, its earlier design, added several new weights to the family, and changed its name to Stymie. Some say that it was given this name as a sly joke because the family was designed to stymie (block and hinder) the flow of European typefaces into America. Stymie found immediate popularity, but it was short-lived because Linotype decided to import Memphis to the United States.

More recent additions to the family of square serif typestyles include ITC Lubalin Graph, A&S Gallatin, Calvert (designed by Margaret Calvert, one of the few women in type design), Glypha, Serifa, and Egyptian 505, which was developed as part of a student design project (the classroom number was 505).

The first square serif face was called Egyptian because early in the nineteenth century, when the first designs were released, there was great public interest in

Memphis

Schedule of Free Activities
November & December 1985

All events will take place
in the Children's Bookshop
on the second floor of the Museum.

....

HOLIDAY
AUTOGRAPHING
....

Weekends at 2 P.M.
Award Winning
Children's Book Illustrators
Will Sign
Your Holiday Gift Books.

Tomie de Paola
Sunday, November 3

Donna Diamond
Saturday, November 9

Jan Brett
Sunday, November 10

Tasha Tudor
Saturday, November 16

Diane Goode
Sunday, November 17

Eric Carle
Saturday, November 23

Arnold Lobel
Sunday, November 24

Jane Breskin Zalben
Saturday, November 30

*Vit Horejs, actor-author
Sunday, December 1

Anita Lobel
Saturday, December 7

Barbara Cooney
(2:30) Sunday, December 8

Petra Mathers
Saturday, December 14

Leo & Diane Dillon
Sunday, December 15

*This event is made possible with public funds
from the literature program
of the New York State Council on the Arts

Memphis Bold and Light typefaces were selected by designer Linda Florio to create this bookmark, printed on both sides, which was typeset by David Seham and Associates.

Egyptian antiquities. Typefoundries chose Egyptian-sounding names in an effort to gain immediate acceptance.

CONSIDERATIONS FOR USE

Memphis can be an exceptionally versatile and forgiving design—except when set too tight. Memphis is a sturdy typeface that provides the clarity of a sans serif with the readability of a serif.

Almost any paper stock is suitable for Memphis. Its stroke and serif weights ensure character integrity on coarse paper, and its lack of apparent weight stress prevents dazzling on coated or colored stock. Memphis is an ideal choice when paper must be inexpensive and readability must be assured.

Also, various graphic techniques, such as reversing type out of blocks of color, halftones, or line art and other effects that would normally impair readability, can be employed with confidence when using square serif typefaces. They generally have few subtleties or delicate parts that would be degraded by these processes.

Although typefaces neither have specific personalities nor evoke particular feelings, copy set in Memphis tends to have a straightforward, no-nonsense kind of appearance. Square serifs are not considered fancy and are rarely considered beautiful, although there is a feeling of elegance to many designs in the lighter weights. They are matter-of-fact designs with just a hint of assertiveness.

There is one drawback to using square serif typestyles: They do not lend themselves to tight letterspacing in text composition because the color of text copy set in these designs is easily disrupted. The monotone character weight, open counters, and serifs, which echo the strokes, all combine to create exceptionally even typographic color. Tight letterspacing will quickly degrade this harmony, especially when two or more characters come so close together that they touch.

Another drawback is that interlocking square serif letters tend to produce unfamiliar character shapes more easily than do other serif typestyles. In other serif typestyles, the serifs are finer and not perceived as an integral part of the letter. When they touch and combine with serifs of other letters, the main character shapes tend to stay dominant. Not so with square serifs. When they are set too tight and serifs touch or interlock, a completely different character is often the result—one that the reader is forced to decipher.

Happily, this is a rarer occurrence in display typography, where tight letterspacing can be a virtue. Generally, as square serif typestyles put on weight, their serifs become shorter in length. The bold and black designs of individual families can usually be set quite tight without serifs touching. In fact, for the most part, these designs make excellent display typefaces. Memphis is no exception. Much like the original square serif designs, it is an excellent attention-getter, has high levels of legibility, uses

space efficiently, and mixes well with a variety of typestyles.

Memphis can provide a pleasing counterplay to the most common text typefaces—whether they are serif or sans serif in design. The only caution is that, like sans serif typefaces, square serifs do not usually work very well when mixing one family with another. If this style of typeface is to be used for both text copy and display heads, both typefaces should be from the same family. The good news is that most families are quite versatile and easy to work with.

A little care should be taken when choosing the weights to be used. For one thing, square serif faces tend to get heavy quite quickly. The book and light weights are ideal for lengthy text copy, but, many times, the medium will create a heavy-looking page of text. This is fine for a less than ideal printing surface but can be uninviting for long blocks of copy on a finer paper stock.

Another area to watch when mixing a sans serif with a square serif design is the weight contrast between the two faces. Generally, it is a good idea to use weights that make this contrast easily apparent.

Finally, when using rules, their weight should be proportional to the character stroke weight. This is a subtlety that, although not necessarily for effective communication or pleasing graphics, helps create a continuity within a design.

Since these typestyles are such effective communicators and so easy to use, it is a wonder that square serifs are not used more often.

Optima

ABCDEFGHIJKLMNOPQRSTUVWXYZ
abcdefghijklmnopqrstuvwxyz
1234567890
$)] - ; / — , . ! ([& - : / ? , . ¢ ¿ ¡ ß £ / — „ ·

ABCDEFGHIJKLMNOPQRSTUVWXYZ
abcdefghijklmnopqrstuvwxyz
1234567890
$)] - ; / — , . ! ([& - : / ? , . ¢ ¿ ¡ ß £ / — „ ·

Optima
Optima Italic
Optima Medium
Optima Medium Italic
Optima Bold
Optima Bold Italic
Optima Black
Optima Black Italic

Hermann Zapf has a problem. The marketing people at Stempel got hold of his favorite typeface and changed its name, and he doesn't like it. The Stempel marketing people felt that Zapf's typeface needed a stronger, more dramatic name than New Antiqua. They picked Optima.

Not only is Optima Zapf's favorite design, it is also his most popular and probably his most original. He calls Optima a "serifless roman"; others have referred to it as a "stressed sans," "humanistic sans," and "calligraphic sans." Zapf's favorite typeface clearly defies simple stereotyping, and to label it as just "distinctive" does not do it justice. In Optima, Zapf has somehow managed to combine the verve of calligraphic writing, the clarity of sans serif letter shapes, and the classic proportions of Roman inscriptional letters. No easy task even for one of the world's most talented type designers.

ATTRIBUTES

Optima is easy to spot—there is no other type quite like it (at least there are no other typefaces similar to Optima that are readily available).

Optima has no serifs, and yet it looks like no other traditional sans serif type. It contains no severe geometric forms, no strict adherence to a system of weights and proportion, no monotone character strokes, and no artificial squaring of counters and bowls. In fact, the only thing Optima shares with other sans serif designs is a lack of those "little feet" at the ends of terminals.

Finding the Right Pigeonhole. Although it is almost always grouped with the likes of Helvetica, Futura, and other sans serif designs, Optima should be considered as an elegant serifless roman. Compare it to Baskerville or Garamond, however, and you will find similar proportions, shapes, and weight stress.

Where these designs have serifs, Optima has a slight flaring of its stroke weight. If the truth were known, Zapf would have preferred to make this flaring even more subtle, but he noticed that other sans serif types had a tendency to lose some of their crispness during a lengthy press run. As a result, he exaggerated his original terminal design to overcome this drawback of metal type composition.

True to its Roman heritage, Optima has wide, full-bodied characters, especially in the capitals. Only the *E, F,* and *L* deviate and have narrow forms. Consistent with almost every other Zapf typeface, the cap *S* in Optima appears top heavy and tilts forward just slightly. The *M* is splayed, and the *N,* like a serif design, has light vertical strokes.

Subtleties in Little Letters. Again, like its Roman cousins, the lowercase *a* and *g* in Optima are two-storied designs. Also in the lowercase, the dots over the *i* and *j* are aligned below the ascender line. Although certainly not necessary for the process of distinguishing Optima from other types, it does contain a number of subtleties that further help to define the design; the lowercase *f* stem thins at the curve, the *t* has a relatively tall ascender topped by an angled terminal, and the ear of the *g* is parallel with the baseline.

One way Optima differs dramatically from serif types and is more closely linked to a Univers or ITC Franklin Gothic is in its italic letterforms. There are no free-flowing, cursive shapes here, no softer expression of the designer's hand. Optima Italic, like most other sans serif designs, is not much more than an inclined roman.

BACKGROUND

World War II marked a turning point in Hermann Zapf's work. Prior to the war his designs showed talent and exceptional ability but none of the special qualities that make his typefaces so important today. It was just after the war and his return to Stempel that he began work on some of the designs for which he is so well known. Palatino and Melior were two of his first works. Work was to begin on Optima some time later. Zapf intended Palatino to be used as a text face for books and publications of substance. Melior was initially drawn as a newspaper face, with readability and legibility of primary design concern.

The work on Optima was not begun with such lofty goals. It was first intended to be a secondary companion to its serifed brethren: a display face to complement Zapf's earlier work. The origins of Optima are, in fact, to be found in his earliest display letterforms.

Busman's Holiday. In the early 1950s, Zapf was able to travel to Italy for a well-earned holiday and to do research on early Italian typeface design. While there, he happened upon some ancient Roman gravestones in Florence. These relics, missed by most tourists and casual observers, delighted Zapf and appealed to his classic sense of design.

Hours were spent sketching the inscribed letterforms. Many drawings were made in Italy, and many, many more back in Zapf's office at Stempel. Work proceeded slowly, partly because Zapf was unclear about the direction the design was to take: a complementary display design or a text face that could stand on its own.

Over the months, the idea for Optima began to take shape. Countless trial sketches and the advice of trusted friends began to show Zapf the correct design path to follow.

Help From Across the Atlantic. Although its roots are in ancient inscriptional letters, the design of Optima was aided by the most advanced technology the 1950s could offer. While working on the basic roman designs, Zapf heard of a progressive typesetting studio in New York that was able to create seemingly magical distortions of type and letterforms through a mysterious photographic process. The type studio was Photo-Lettering, and the magician was Ed Rondthaler, the father of photographic design distortions.

Zapf contacted Rondthaler and asked if he could perform a little of his magic on the initial renderings for Optima. Zapf knew that he wanted his italic to be

Optima

an obliqued roman rather than a true cursive; but he also knew that this seemingly simple design exercise demanded just as much time and effort as drawing a completely new design. His goal in contacting Rondthaler was to determine if the then new technology of photographic distortion could be harnessed successfully as a design tool.

The result for Zapf was absolute success. Although the finished photographic

Designers Alan Mickelson and Clint Hansen selected Optima for this poster because it suggested the past—ship posters of the 1920s and 1930s employed similar styles— yet the face had a contemporary feel.

distortion provided by Photo-Lettering was a very long way from being a completed type design, it did save Zapf hundreds of preliminary sketches and trial drawings.

The first sketches of Optima were made in 1952, but it wasn't until 1958 that the first weights of the family were made available as Linotype matrices— and this was only in Europe. It was another two years before American designers could specify Hermann Zapf's favorite typeface.

Not Everybody's Favorite. As popular as Optima has been with typographers and graphic communicators, it has never been a favorite among manufacturers of type composition equipment. In fact, it has been nothing but a series of headaches. Since Optima was virtually an instant success, all vendors of typesetting equipment and type fonts were obligated to include it as part of their product offering. This was no problem, but when they approached Linotype with requests to license the design, each was met with a resounding "No!" They then had a choice: remain ethical but uncompetitive, and not release Optima, or fudge a little on ethics (but maintain acceptable legal standards) and release the design under a different name.

Unfortunately, the rest is history. Zapf was denied the royalties that would normally be due him because the various type manufacturers were forced to copy his work from second generation prints (and usually by designers with considerably less talent than Zapf) and because some members of the design community were forced to live with the less than ideal designs from many of its suppliers.

Optima has also been a technological headache. It was originally created for metal type composition, and since it is his favorite design, Zapf was obviously pleased with the result. He has not, however, been happy with any technological version of Optima since the original. He was not involved with Linotype's process

of conversion from metal matrices to second generation photo type fonts and believes that the results could have been better. In addition, early photo type composition was output on film and paper that not only failed to do justice to the design, but actually obliterated much of Optima's basic character traits.

Then along came digital type, with its imaging technology that produces exceptionally clear, crisp shapes. But it also produces straight lines much better than it does curves—especially of the subtle sort found in Optima. As a result, digital versions of Optima, particularly those of relatively coarse resolution or those that are output at normal text sizes, are too often only poor caricatures of Zapf's original intention. Zapf has said many times that he would never have designed Optima if he were limited to digital technology. For now, graphic communicators can only hope that one day soon type imaging equipment will do justice to the face.

CONSIDERATIONS FOR USE

Many purists would argue that Optima should be avoided until typesetting equipment can do a more successful job of duplicating the original design. Although it would be a tragedy to see Optima's demise as a communications tool, at the same time an insistence on using this type under poor conditions benefits no one. When and when not to use Optima should be made on a case by case basis, with careful regard for typesetting technology, point size, and the quality of the basic design. Unfortunately, these are not easy decisions, nor are there any handy guidelines for making the correct choice. The key is to use your eye. Look at the version you intend to use. Does it accurately reflect the subtle beauty of Zapf's original? To the degree it does, you are safe in using it.

Once the initial hurdle of whether or not to use Optima has been cleared, the rest is relatively easy. Optima requires only basic care to produce beautiful and efficient communication.

Optima can be used in a wide variety of applications. It is ideal for short blocks of copy and, unlike most sans serif faces, can be used with confidence in lengthy text composition. Its slight swelling at the ends of terminals provides an adequate alternative to serifs in guiding the eye across the page, and its stressed stroke weights never tire the eye, as do many more monotone designs. Optima may not be an ideal text face—but it comes very close. It can also be set advantageously in almost any size. Billboards, box tops, brochures, and books have all been set in Optima. It is only in the smallest sizes that Optima begins to lose some of its strength. And if you choose to use Optima for very small copy, there is even a version designed specifically for this purpose—although you will have to look long and hard to find a typographer who makes this version available.

Advantages of Being a Sans. Because it is a sans, Optima benefits from generous line spacing. If your layout allows such a luxury, take advantage of this trait. There are virtually no limits to the amount of white space that can be added between lines of text. As an example, Zapf once created an exceptionally lovely and highly readable book using Optima set 9 on 24 point.

Good versions of Optima are excellent communicators, and the added benefit is that they perform with beauty and grace.

Like most sans serifs, Optima also benefits from a wide range of letterspacing capabilities. It can be set quite tight, with spacing as established by the font vendor (which is usually the best), or evenly letterspaced with enough room between letters to allow a Mack truck to make a U-turn. If there are any guidelines, Optima should be set more open than tight. It is not that readability is affected that much when Optima is set on

The logo for NOA International, Inc., a company with a Swedish heritage, required a face that was clean and crisp like Swedish design. Designer Kurt Meinecke thus selected Optima; the face balances the classic beauty of a serif with the simplicity of a sans serif.

the snug side; it is just that the unhurried elegance and light "gray" color created by the face is disrupted by letters that are set too tight. Again, this is an eye judgment that will vary depending on application, point size, and paper stock.

Mixability. Optima is about as gregarious as a typeface can get. It mixes well with virtually any serif design and a surprisingly wide range of sans serif faces.

Optima combines exceptionally well with any other type designed by Hermann Zapf. It mixes with Melior and Palatino; this was one of Zapf's design goals. It will also support any other Zapf design. There is a similarity, an underlying quality, that is apparent in all of Zapf's typestyles. Critics (most of whom do not design type) like to criticize Zapf ,for this characteristic. Graphic communicators should thank him, however, because it assures them that all of Zapf's designs can be combined at will—with beautiful results.

Optima also mixes well with a large variety of non-Zapf designs. With serif faces, Optima is a natural, and even most sans serifs seem to work well with this

serifless face. Faces as diverse as Baskerville, Trump Mediaeval, and Helvetica all combine exceptionally well with Optima.

There are just two areas in which some caution should be exercised. First, do not mix Optima with other typefaces that have somewhat similar terminals. (Be careful with designs like Americana and Albertus.) Second, avoid sans serifs like Frutiger and Syntax, which have an obvious calligraphic heritage. Optima combined with faces such as these can create an unpleasant visual tension.

Availability. Optima is available in a range of four weights plus companion italics: The Roman is elegant but somewhat light for small sizes and a few other applications; the Medium is fine for everything but lacks a little of the Roman's grace; the Bold works as an excellent text emphasizer; and the Black is a superior display design—powerful, without becoming a caricature of the lighter weights.

Once you get past the fact that not all Optimas are created equal, Hermann Zapf's favorite typeface is nothing but good news. It is beautiful, distinctive, versatile, and an excellent communicator.

Palatino

ABCDEFGHIJKLMNOPQRSTUVWXYZ
abcdefghijklmnopqrstuvwxyz
1234567890
$)] - ; / — , . ! ([& - : / ? , . ¢ ¿ ¡ ß £/— „ ·

ABCDEFGHIJKLMNOPQRSTUVWXYZ
abcdefghijklmnopqrstuvwxyz
1234567890
$)] - ; / — , . ! ([& - : / ? , . ¢ ¿ ¡ ß £/— „ ·

Palatino
Palatino Italic
Palatino Bold
Palatino Bold Italic

Hermann Zapf is an unassuming, gentle man. He never boasts about the beautiful books and graphics he produces and rarely even talks about his typeface designs. Only if pressed will he answer any questions about his type (much as a proud but modest father would speak about his children). Palatino, though, has held a special place for Zapf since it was first released in 1950. In fact, the young Zapf seriously considered using Palatino to set his wedding announcement. He chose, however, a "competitor type": Diotima, designed by his bride, Gudrun von Hesse.

ATTRIBUTES

Palatino is classified as an Old Style design. Palatino conforms to most Old Style traits—obliqued weight stress, head serifs that are angled, foot serifs that tend to be free-form—except that it has a little more stroke weight contrast than most Old Styles. As a result, Palatino has been called "an Old Style with the brightness of Bodoni." Most Old Style design traits, such as angled head serifs and oblique weight stress, have no real bearing on typeface legibility or readability, but stroke weight contrast does.

Palatino also differs from typical Old Style designs in that its counters are open and its overall proportions are expanded. Both these traits help Palatino remain legible and readable under a variety of printing and reading conditions.

Energetic Yet Disciplined. There is a particular charm to Palatino. It has verve, vitality, and almost a sense of innocence; traits found in few types, especially few German types. Zapf based his design of Palatino on the work of sixteenth-century Italian writing masters, and it is obviously shown in the finished work's classical proportions and grace. Subtle curves (as found in the final stroke of the *n*) and robust compound shapes (like

those in the cap and lowercase *s*) are melded expertly in this most energetic of Zapf's type designs. Yet underlying all these calligraphic traits is the discipline and strength that is typical of German typeface design. The end result is a type that is exceptionally lively and yet has the control to perform in a variety of applications (sort of a Times Roman with personality).

Individual Characters. Palatino's most used character, the lowercase *e*, benefits from an exceptionally large counter for an Old Style design (no filling here). Foot serifs on the final strokes of the *h*, *m*, and *n* are on the outside only. These are more like the natural calligraphic termination of a stroke than the typographically common double-sided serif. Calligraphic shapes also show up in a variety of other characters: the bowl of the capital *D* pulls to the upper right, as do those of the *P* and *R*. The tail of the *y* and the heavy diagonal of the *x* were also obviously influenced by hand-drawn brush strokes. Finally, there is Palatino's calligraphic hallmark: the unusually curved yet somehow elegant spine of the *s*.

A high crossbar to the cap *A*, the splayed *Y,* and the relatively tall *t* also help to distinguish Palatino from less-personable designs. In all, Palatino is easy to spot. It is the pretty face.

BACKGROUND

Contrary to popular belief, Palatino is not Hermann Zapf's first typeface—but it is his first commercially successful typeface.

Zapf's first type was a typical German black letter called Gilgengart. Although already an accomplished calligrapher at the age of twenty, Zapf had yet to learn the art of typeface design. Gilgengart was to serve as his type design primer. As a result, the face developed slowly and was plagued with many false starts and dead-

ends. As Zapf wrote later, "A new printing type has a long, often thorny, way to completion. Before a type has come far enough to please outsiders, it adds gray hairs to its coproducers." Gilgengart probably added its fair share of gray hairs but was eventually cut in two versions. The completed design never attained any significant degree of popularity, however. In all fairness, this was more because black letter fell into disfavor rather than because of any lack of ability on the part of the young Zapf.

In 1941, Zapf was conscripted into the German army and served as a cartographer in France—first in Dijon and later in Bordeaux. Always an optimist, Zapf found the time, and a place in his heart, to begin a set of flower drawings during the height of his military service. These were saved and later enlarged upon after the war. The final result was published as "Das Blumen-ABC" (flower alphabet) by Stempel in 1948.

The Beginnings. On his return from France (and the war), Zapf was hired by the Stempel typefoundry to help them rebuild their type library. In 1946, he began work on a new roman with the working name Novalis. Trial cuttings were made in the 10-point size, but the face was not to reach completion. At the same time Zapf had been working on Novalis, he was also producing some trial sketches on a display type that was softer and more charismatic than its predecessor. Zapf showed these drawings to the Stempel management, and it was immediately agreed that the second design was, by far, the better of the two. Thus, all work on Novalis was abandoned, and Zapf concentrated on completing the face that was first called Medici, then Palatino, after the sixteenth-century Italian writing master Giovambattista Palatino.

Palatino was virtually an instant success. Production could barely keep up with the demand for the handset type

Palatino

and the slightly different Linotype composing matrices. Some years later, when it came time to produce phototype fonts for the Linofilm typesetter, a difficult decision had to be made. Mike Parker, who was then director of typographic development at Mergenthaler Linotype, wrote: "Hand-set Palatino had always had a restless look to my eye. When we came to cut Linofilm Palatino, I asked Hermann Zapf what version he thought we should work from. He replied that he thought neither the existing machine versions of Palatino nor the hand-set version was as good as they might be—but that a photo composition version of Palatino with some of the discipline of 'Aldus' [a special book face designed by Zapf in 1954] might be the best possible Palatino. This we commissioned him to do, and the result is Linofilm Palatino."

Unfortunately, though Palatino was the first of Zapf's faces to reach popularity, it is also probably the first of his designs to be copied. Until very recently, Mergenthaler Linotype had a strict company policy against cross-licensing of its typeface designs. As a result of this non-license policy, manufacturers of competing typographic composition equipment were forced to copy the design of Palatino (and many other Zapf designs) to remain competitive in the marketplace. Early on, not many of the Linotype's competitors were very good copiers; as a result, the majority of the typographic community was compelled to live with poor design copies.

Over the years, much better versions of Palatino have been produced. Designers and typographers can now benefit from almost universally good versions of the most popular faces. Unfortunately, Zapf must continue to live with the fact that his typeface has been kidnapped.

Sandra McHenry of Pentagram Design, Inc.'s San Francisco office chose Palatino for this job for the Mt. Everest Expedition because she wanted a classical face that would integrate well with the art and capture the soaring quality of Mt. Everest.

CONSIDERATIONS FOR USE

Because of its versatility, or perhaps because of its popularity, Palatino has been used in every imaginable typographic application. For most of these it performs admirably. It is not, however, a universal typestyle.

Palatino is an obvious typeface; it has a strong personality that almost cannot go unnoticed, even by the typographically unaware. Palatino makes a statement; a beautiful statement, but a statement nonetheless. Mundane typography can be set in Palatino, but simple directories, blocks of documentation, reference material, and like applications somehow end up looking a little overdressed when set in Palatino. It has also become the typeface of choice when typographic novices want a face that looks pretty or when they want to evoke feelings of refinement or sophistication. Although Palatino is exceptionally beautiful and is both a refined and a remarkably sophisticated design, it also borders on overuse in obvious or, too often, wrong applications.

Yet Palatino is a valuable and still remarkably versatile addition to any graphic communicator's typographic palette. Palatino's wide proportions and open counters ensure that it remains readable at all but microscopic type sizes and on a wide variety of paper stocks. The distinctive character shapes that give the face its personality also provide for high levels of typographic legibility. Even though it is not a Century Schoolbook, no one is going to have trouble reading copy set in Palatino.

Sparkle Without Dazzle. Palatino's moderate degree of stroke weight contrast works to its best interest. There is just enough to add some sparkle to a page.

This helps maintain reader attention (the eye actually needs some relatively obvious stroke contrast to maintain reasonable interest levels). Palatino's weight contrast is obvious, but it is nowhere near the point of causing any dazzling problems.

Because its proportions are slightly expanded, there is a lot of air on the insides of characters (Palatino has quite open counters). This is good in that it improves typeface readability—but only if the face is set with ample letterspacing. Palatino does not like to be set tight. As the optical space between letters becomes less than that inside the letters, the face begins to lose some of its naturally even color, and readability begins to suffer. Palatino is an expansive face; let it breathe.

Palatino's Special Italic. The italic, because of its narrower proportions, can be set tighter. Even though the stroke weight of Palatino italic is markedly lighter than the roman, when set tight, the general color of the design becomes darker. The end result is that it melds perfectly with the roman to create exceptionally even page color. Palatino italic is a particularly beautiful design in its own right.

Palatino can be mixed with just about any other typeface. It contrasts well with virtually any sans serif design and even complements a variety of serif types. Two points of caution here: Palatino can clash with some Old Style designs (pick one with very different design traits—like ITC Weidemann), and it does not get on well with other designs with a strong personality. Palatino and Antique Olive, or Palatino and ITC Souvenir, for example, would probably not be especially good mixes. The sturdiness of Rockwell or ITC Lubalin Graph would, however,

contrast nicely with Palatino's sensuous proportions. Helvetica, especially the Inserat designs, would make dynamic heads when combined with Palatino in text. Or, you might try the marriage of Palatino and Diotima.

Long Lines Are No Problem. Because of its expanded proportions, Palatino can, and in many cases should, have long line lengths. This is a face that can do a good job of filling out a measure. It is also one of those styles that does not tire the eye when longer line lengths are specified. The other side of the coin is that Palatino does not perform at its best in short lines—especially if they are set justified. (Do not set newspapers in Palatino.)

Palatino comes from a relatively small family; originally it was released in only three variants—roman, italic, and bold. However, swash characters were added early on for the italic design. Later still, a bold italic was added to the family. In fact, these four weights still comprise the complete Palatino family as available from most sources.

Useful Accessories. Shortly after finishing the initial Palatino designs, Zapf also drew two sets of exceptionally handsome titling caps: Michelangelo and Sistina. (Titling faces are all-cap designs usually drawn to fill the full point-body in metal type. Unfortunately, first with photo, and now digital type, these faces tend to be going the way of old cars on the East Coast and $5.00 movie tickets.) Michelangelo is a slender and almost delicate design; Sistina is more on the robust side. Both are good display type tools, but they are a little hard to find.

It is easy to see why Zapf's Palatino has also become the favorite of many graphic communicators. It is distinctive, beautiful, and exceptionally versatile.

Plantin

ABCDEFGHIJKLMNOPQRSTUVWXYZ
abcdefghijklmnopqrstuvwxyz
1234567890
$)] - ; / — , . ! ([& - : / ? , . ¢ ¿ ¡ ß £ / — „ ·

ABCDEFGHIJKLMNOPQRSTUVWXYZ
abcdefghijklmnopqrstuvwxyz
1234567890
$)] - ; / — , . ! ([& - : / ? , . ¢ ¿ ¡ ß £ / — „ ·

Plantin Light
Plantin Light Italic
Plantin
Plantin Italic
Plantin Bold
Plantin Bold Italic
Plantin Bold Condensed

The typographic community has a history of trying to do the right thing. There are pirates and scoundrels in our ranks, like anywhere else, but they are very much in the minority. For one thing, we always try to give credit when it is due—which is why so many typefaces are named after their designer—an admirable tradition. Unfortunately, this practice is only admirable as long as the correct name is associated with the type. If it is not, the results are confusing. Type folk may have their hearts in the right place, but unfortunately, they do not always have their facts correct.

As a result, we have typefaces like Garamond, which was named for a very important and influential French printer—but by someone who not only did not design but never even used the types bearing that name. Then there is Janson, which was not developed by the Dutch typographer Nicholas Janson, but by the Hungarian Nicholas Kis. Not the last, nor the least confusing, of these typographical malapropisms is Plantin. Christopher Plantin, a Frenchman who worked in Holland, should be remembered and honored, as he was instrumental in helping to create the rich typographical tradition we enjoy today. He was to a large degree responsible for making Dutch type and typography the model of sixteenth-century printing. He never, however, used the types named after him.

ATTRIBUTES

Even at a glance, two traits of the Plantin typeface are immediately apparent. First, it is a "big-boned" typeface—just a little on the heavy side. Second, it can say a lot in relatively little space (because it is slightly condensed). Plantin is a pioneer of sorts, being one of the first typefaces designed with durability and economy of space as primary functional aspects. Some typeface design traits are just that: traits, which are only useful in their ability to help distinguish one type design from another; but other aspects provide real benefits to the graphic communicator. Plantin's weight and condensed proportions fall into the latter category.

Plantin also has a relatively tall x-height—another aspect that works in the design's favor. It can be used with the assurance that readability standards are easily met. Even at small sizes, Plantin makes a strong visual statement.

Like the rest of the design, Plantin's serifs are strong and just slightly heavy. Head serifs on the lowercase ascending strokes are wedge-shaped in the Old Style tradition, and the baseline counterparts look more like something you would find in Bookman or Clarendon. They are forceful, with heavy bracketing, and have square-cut ends; the kind that are ideal for holding up under adverse printing and reading conditions.

Being classified as a Dutch Old Style, Plantin has an oblique weight stress and relatively little contrast in stroke thickness. Although these two traits do not necessarily provide any qualitative typographic benefits, it is said by some that Old Style designs allow for more distinctive character shapes than many other serif types, and that this can help character legibility levels. In addition, the relatively even stroke weights in Old Styles can produce a uniform typographic color that is inviting to the reader and creates less "show-through" on lightweight stock.

Traits that allow you to spot or identify Plantin also abound. These are the kind that make the design distinctive, but probably do little to affect typography. These are the "bird-watcher" traits—fun, but not functional. The easiest way to spot Plantin in a crowd is to look for its characteristic flat-topped A. It looks as if the designer made the right stroke of the letter in one broad movement, intending to come back later and cut it back to proper length with the sixteenth-century version of correction fluid—and then forgot to do so. The diagonal of the italic capital N also echoes this trait, but an italic N is more difficult to find than the roman cap A.

Other characteristics of Plantin include the splayed cap M and the sheared terminals of the C, G, and S. In both the roman and the italic, the bowl of the P does not quite close. If you get a chance to view or use the italics, you will probably also notice that the capital J is a little out of character. It is the only decorative (or swash) cap letter and can be confused with an F.

The lowercase descenders are short and counters are open. The a is distinctive in that the top terminal is square-cut and begins to turn in on the character. The bottom diagonal of the k is blunt, and in some versions of the face, the character appears a little top-heavy. The italic v,w, and z have just a little panache as a result of their swash-like characteristics. This last trait and the extension of the top of the p through its main stroke doesn't disrupt the design, but they're a little out of character with the other letters.

All of this makes Plantin a typically strong northern-European typestyle—one that is well suited to harsh typographic climates and short spans of reader attention.

BACKGROUND

By the early twentieth century, Linotype and Monotype composing machines had firmly established themselves as practical typographic tools. Most large print shops and publishing houses had at least one or two of these nineteenth-century works of industrial art on their premises. But, as with so many innovations, these new composing machines were able to produce only results that looked like previous technologies. Type development was bound by the "wing-walking" theory of change, which dictates that you do not let go of one technology until you have a very firm grip on the next. (It is the kind of thinking that gave us television programs that were often nothing more than old radio shows with pictures, as well as plastic that is produced to look like wood or leather.) For the first couple of decades of machine composition, typefaces made available for this equipment were little more than the old hand-set faces forced to work by gears and levels.

Then, in the first part of this century,

Plantin

Linotype and Monotype ran out of nineteenth-century typefaces to copy. Typographic innovation became an important aspect of the services that equipment suppliers offered to their customers. The design and release of Plantin was one of the first steps taken to supply typographers and printers with something new in type.

Most text and reference books credit F. H. Pierpont as the designer responsible for the modern revival of Plantin. Actually, Pierpont did not draw the face—in fact, he was not a type designer at all. Pierpont was the production manager of Pierpont and Steltzer, a large British printing and publishing house. He did not design Plantin, but it was his passion and guidance that made the design happen.

Early in the century, Monotype released Imprint, a typeface designed for the periodical of the same name. Pierpont was impressed with the typeface for several reasons. It was a good design—it was also the first innovative face from Monotype—and it was created to satisfy the needs of one company. Pierpont thought, if Monotype could produce a face for *Imprint* magazine, why not a face for his company? He had long felt that his work would benefit from a face that was distinctive, legible, and could print well on both coated and coarse papers. A visit to Antwerp, prompted by his manager's interest in printing history, spurred Pierpont's interest in the project and gave him the idea for the basic design. He saw at Antwerp's Plantin Museum the exquisite collection of sixteenth-century punches and matrices used by Christopher Plantin.

In the museum, an alert technician like Pierpont could find examples and documentation of the various stages of type manufacture. This, and the enthusiasm of Max Rooses (the first director of the repository), was all the encouragement Pierpont needed to use this resource as the basis for his work. Pierpont left the museum with a wealth of knowledge, hundreds of photographs, and stacks of antique typeset specimens—including a few examples of Robert Granjon's that were produced by the Plantin Press but never used by its founder. These were to become the premise for Pierpont's design.

He took his portfolio of Dutch types to the Monotype works, and under his direction, an adaptation was drawn and pantographically cut. In adapting the antique types for contemporary needs, Pierpont and the Monotype craftsmen mixed a love and understanding of sixteenth-century type with a healthy dose of poetic license. In fact, when they were finished, the design had as much in common with a nineteenth-century Clarendon as with a sixteenth-century Granjon. The classic Old Style text design was preserved in the basic structure, but newfound strength and body were added to the delicate frame. The combination was deliberate—and successful. Shortly after it was released, a number of typographically influential presses adopted Monotype Plantin, and as a result, it became the typeface of choice in virtually all kinds of printing (sort of the Helvetica of its day).

Plantin turned out to be such an exceptional communications tool that Stanley Morison used it as the basis for the design of Times New Roman. A comparison of these two seemingly diverse designs will show a remarkable resemblance. Color is almost identical, proportions are the same; in fact, Times looks like a Plantin on a diet.

Most current graphic-arts equipment suppliers offer good versions of Plantin, but because it is not a particularly popular design in the United States, only the larger type shops generally have fonts. This is unfortunate, because Plantin is a good design that deserves to be used more. Svelte (at least in typography) is not always a required trait.

CONSIDERATIONS FOR USE

The trick to using Plantin is to remember that it is a heavy face. Give it room to breathe, do not get too complicated in typographic arrangement, and mix it carefully with other designs. This may seem like a lot of negatives, but you should not consider Plantin a difficult face with which to work. Actually, most of the guidelines for using this face fall into the category of common sense—and the rewards for using Plantin correctly are worth the effort.

The most inviting and easy-to-use text copy is typographically even and light gray in color. Text copy that is dark, on the other hand, appears ponderous to the reader. Although Plantin is no flyweight, it need not look heavy. Just be sure to: (1) keep letterspacing within reasonable limits; (2) complement the letterspacing with line space that does not cramp the design; and (3) mix Plantin with typefaces that balance or offset its weight, not those that add to it.

Since Plantin is a little chunky, a certain amount of care should be taken when tight-set typography is ordered. Actually, it is one of those faces that does not benefit from creativity in spacing—Plantin works just fine right out of the box. Its serifs are not especially long, so premature lock-up is not a problem; but when two round characters (like an *od* combination) come close together, they cause a dark spot in the copy that is distracting to the eye and can even disrupt reading. For the most part, Plantin should be set with the spacing intended by the type manufacturer. Virtually every available version shows that it was designed—and spaced—with exceptional care.

Display sizes provide more opportunity to play around with spacing. In larger sizes, Plantin benefits from a little custom spacing. Its shapes are quite distinctive and somewhat demanding. Custom spacing, which is usually on the tight side, can produce some surprising, dynamic graphics.

The short descenders in Plantin help maintain even typographic color in text copy. They provide for some natural line space when the typeface is set solid or with little leading. Plantin needs this. If it is set with too little line space, the resulting block of copy will look dark. At small text sizes, 10 point and below,

Plantin's natural line spacing is sufficient. As you go up in size to the 16-, 18-, and 24-point sizes, which are not popular for blocks of advertising text copy, this natural line space may need a little extra help. How much additional line space you specify will depend on things like the application, the number of lines in the copy block, paper stock, and so on. Just remember that copy that is optically heavy and dark will not entice readers or do anything positive for readability.

For just a couple of lines of display copy, you are on your own. Necessary line spacing may vary dramatically according to the length of line or even the individual characters used. At times, the mechanical spacing among a group of lines should change from line to line. The Golden Rule in typography is that things should look right rather than measure consistently.

Like folks with strong personalities, Plantin does not necessarily mix well with all typographic partners—and it likes to dominate most group functions. The first hint when combining Plantin with other designs is to stay in the family if possible. Mix Plantin roman with its bold and italic counterparts. You might even ask your typographer to provide you with a slight electronic modification (embold the bold a little more or condense the roman slightly). Because of its strength, Plantin can survive distortions (as long as they are subtle) better than many other designs. You cannot go wrong mixing a Plantin with a Plantin.

If the well-worn path is not yours, and you must mix different typestyles, then combine Plantin with a style that will complement it or dramatically highlight its design traits. Because their designs have a common root, Plantin and Times Roman, Plantin and Garamond, or Plantin and ITC Galliard should not be combined. The delicacy of Goudy Old Style or the clinical coolness of Bodoni, however, would complement the robust, strong-willed character of Plantin.

Just about any sans serif will also combine well with Plantin. ITC Avant Garde Gothic, Helvetica, and Frutiger will all

Bob Kwait, creative director for Phillips-Ramsey, San Diego, chose Plantin for this billboard because he wanted a sophisticated face that would transcend distance yet still portray the fun and status of the San Diego Zoo. "The serifs are visible without being too crude, which gives it a gutsy, yet classy style," explains Kwait.

work well in almost any application. A condensed Helvetica or the book weight of ITC Avant Garde Gothic could be a fun combination to try sometime. Experiment with Plantin—you might be very surprised (and very pleased) with the results.

Plantin is a somewhat condensed design, so you will get lots of information into a given space. That is the good news. The bad news is that if you specify wide columns, you will get too many characters on a line. (Readers are only supposed to like about forty characters per line. Do not overfeed them.) With Plantin, you have the benefit of being able to say a lot in relatively little space and at the same time of providing readers with expanses of comfortable and inviting white space.

There are no size restrictions on Plantin. Use it as big or as little as you wish. It is readable and robust at small sizes and performs exceptionally well as a headline face. It can even be used at sizes where type is measured in feet rather than points!

Plantin works in black, in white, and in color. Just about all typefaces work best when they are shown as black images on white paper. Some can perform equally well in a color if the color is

heavy and dark. Few typefaces can be reversed and fewer still can survive being printed in light or pastel colors. Then there is Plantin: It reverses with ease—and with virtually no loss of communication power. It shines in strong colors and performs, as well as can be expected of any type, in light or soft colors. If the job calls for color, think of Plantin.

Not many typefaces are limitless in their range of applications, and unfortunately, those that seem to be are the ones we complain about seeing and having to use too much. Try Plantin. Its range of use is just about as wide as Times Roman and Helvetica, and it still has a freshness to it (even though its basic design predates them both by many, many years). Use Plantin for lengthy, running text, for short blocks that must be highly readable in large or very large sizes. Use it when you are using coarse paper or when color is an important aspect of the communication process. Use Plantin when other faces would be too weak or delicate. Use it to express strength and solidity, or when you want an everyday, mundane piece of work to look just a little "left of center."

Plantin's name may not be entirely accurate, but its typographic aim is.

ITC Souvenir

ABCDEFGHIJKLMNOPQRSTUVWXYZ
abcdefghijklmnopqrstuvwxyz
1234567890
$)] - ; / — , . ! ([& - : / ? , . ¢ ¿ ¡ ß £ / — „ ·

ABCDEFGHIJKLMNOPQRSTUVWXYZ
abcdefghijklmnopqrstuvwxyz
1234567890
$)] - ; / — , . ! ([& - : / ? , . ¢ ¿ ¡ ß £ / — „ ·

ITC Souvenir Light

ITC Souvenir Light Italic

ITC Souvenir Medium

ITC Souvenir Medium Italic

ITC Souvenir Demi

ITC Souvenir Demi Italic

ITC Souvenir Bold

ITC Souvenir Bold Italic

ITC Souvenir Bold Outline

"Nice guys finish last" is, unfortunately, all too often more than just a cliché—it is frequently a true statement. The quiet-spoken, gentle, unassuming people of this world are often overshadowed and overpowered by those more aggressive and dynamic. So it is with people—so it is with type.

ITC Souvenir is a typographic "nice guy": friendly, gentle, unassuming—and it, too, almost finished last. The typestyle was first shown in 1920, along with a number of other designs, in a small specimen booklet issued by ATF. Souvenir was shown again in ATF's famous 1923 specimen book, but it was overshadowed by the first complete showing of their Garamond, Century Schoolbook, and Cloister families. This exceptionally large specimen book, because of its size, could afford to be generous when it came to showing ATF's more popular typefaces. Thirty-three pages were devoted to the Cheltenham family, thirteen pages to Bodoni, twelve to Clearface. Caslon got sixty pages. Souvenir had two.

And that was virtually the end of Souvenir for almost the next fifty years. ATF never showed it again in any of its specimen books. Almost no one purchased it in foundry type, and fewer still used it as a communications tool. The friendly but unassuming Souvenir was almost lost from the typographic repertoire.

Attributes

ITC Souvenir is a soft, undemanding typestyle. It has no sharp edges, no strong contrast in stroke thickness, and virtually no right angles. ITC Souvenir is like a Times Roman dipped in chocolate.

The lowercase is round and large, with several distinctive characters. Much like an Old Style design, the bowl of the *e* has a diagonal stress and the crossbar is on an angle rather than a straight horizontal stroke. In the capitals, the crossbars of the *B* and the *R* are angled rather than horizontal, lending a little art nouveau distinction to these characters.

There are several typographic benefits to these design traits. ITC Souvenir's large x-height and open counters provide for high levels of character legibility and readability throughout the point-size range. Its distinctive characters are also easy to recognize and differentiate from each other, which further extends the typeface's legibility level. ITC Souvenir's soft edges and round corners are kind to most printing surfaces and thus increase its range of usability. ITC Souvenir will print well on newsprint at 6 point and on coated stock at 148 point. Finally, ITC Souvenir has a personality; its lack of hard edges and sharp corners combined with its other design traits, and some almost humorous character forms, give ITC Souvenir a friendly, wholesome quality.

Background

Souvenir is the handiwork of Morris Fuller Benton, ATF's first, most prolific, and probably most famous director of typeface development. A close look at Souvenir reveals subtle design similarities to other Benton designs, such as Clearface, Hobo, and Cheltenham. He drew Souvenir in 1914 as a single-weight design with no italic to complement it. The face was only shown twice by ATF, and no mention of the design is to be found in any of the company's records that survive. Souvenir did not fall from popularity—it never became popular.

Apparently, few orders were placed for fonts of the hand-set type. It never was adapted to machine composition of metal type. Souvenir lay dormant for over forty years, until phototypography gave it a second chance.

In 1967, Photo-Lettering revived the Souvenir design as an exclusive advertising face for one of its accounts. Two years later, the exclusivity of Souvenir was no longer an issue, and Photo-Lettering was able to offer the typestyle to the general public. About this time, another version of Souvenir was drawn for the exclusive

use of Eastern Air Lines. This second version, which is still available from Visual Graphics Corporation under the name of Eastern Souvenir, is somewhat more condensed than the ITC version and is available in only three weights and has no italic designs.

In 1971, ITC was formed and, with the help of Photo-Lettering, introduced ITC Souvenir as one of its first typeface families. It was released in four weights, with corresponding italic designs—all designed by Edward Benguiat. Coincidentally, at this same time, Varityper released a similar version of Souvenir under the guidance of Whedon Davis, their director of typeface development, who had recently left a similar position at ATF.

Like its predecessor, ITC Souvenir did not become an immediate success. This is, however, where similarities in popularity cease. Over a period of several years, ITC Souvenir did gain in popularity. Soon virtually every manufacturer of photocomposition equipment was offering the design as part of its type product line. Typesetting firms bought the type, and graphic communicators specified it. Today, ITC Souvenir is one of ITC's most popular and successful offerings.

It is still bought and used by the graphic design community and has even found its way into the office and electronic publishing environments. ITC Souvenir is available as digital type for graphic arts typesetting, on dry-transfer lettering sheets, and on two-inch film fonts for display composition; it is also available on laser and dot-matrix printers and even on fully formed character printers for office correspondence.

Considerations for Use

There is a common complaint among many art directors and graphic designers that sounds something like this: "There is too much _____ being used. Everywhere you look, you see _____. I am sick of _____ and I will never use it

Recital of
Romantic Italian Music

Given by

MR. JOHN M. LIVERMORE

Under the auspices and direction of the Sophomore
Class of Bellwood University
November twenty-seventh at eight-thirty

Music Hall

This is the first of a series of six recitals to be given by Mr. Livermore during the winter

Thirty-three pages of ATF's famous 1923 specimen book were devoted to Cheltenham. Caslon got sixty pages. Souvenir received only two, which included this modest sample.

again!" You can fill in the blanks with any of a number of typefaces: Helvetica, Times Roman, Goudy Old Style, Century—and ITC Souvenir. There are typefaces that can easily be used too much: typefaces that do not wear well, that are not especially readable or very legible, and that have a narrow range of applications or must be treated with kid gloves to produce reasonably acceptable results. Thankfully, these typefaces are not used too much. (Many probably should not be used at all.) Typefaces like Helvetica, Times Roman, and ITC Souvenir, however, are used so much because they do their jobs so well. They are excellent communications tools. Saying that they are used too much is roughly akin to saying that hammers are used too much for driving nails.

The other side of the coin is that for every typeface there are circumstances or applications that require a little extra attention or care—even for such typefaces as Times Roman, Helvetica, and ITC Souvenir.

ITC Souvenir does not mix as well with Old Style designs as it does with others. It shares too many design traits with these kinds of alphabets to mix easily. Therefore, if you plan to mix ITC Souvenir with a typeface like Goudy Old Style or Garamond, it should be done with care; for example, their weights could be obviously, or even dramatically, different from each other.

No one has ever called ITC Souvenir a sophisticated or particularly elegant design. ITC Souvenir is more "just folks." As a result, you may want to think twice

about choosing it for typography that must be especially elegant. ITC Souvenir Light can be handled so that it takes on a definite air of refinement, but it is never going to reach the levels of sophistication so evident in Bodoni or Spencerian Script.

Outside of the ultraelegant areas, there are virtually no bounds to ITC Souvenir's range of applications and uses. Annual reports, advertisements, menus, magazine text, brochures, price lists, house organs, greeting cards, singage, and even typewritten correspondence fall within its capabilities. Think of an application, and ITC Souvenir can be used for it.

ITC Souvenir works well at very small sizes, at very large sizes, and on a variety of printing surfaces. There is no problem of counters filling in or character shapes becoming unrecognizable. And since serifs are strong and already rounded, virtually no degradation will occur here. ITC Souvenir prints exceptionally well on coated stock, and yet it has the power to withstand the rigors of newsprint.

Except perhaps for some Old Style designs, ITC Souvenir extends its friendly nature to mixing with other typestyles. Sans serifs are a natural; their crisp edges, straight corners, and geometric shapes contrast strikingly with ITC Souvenir's soft humanistic characteristics. This contrast can be further intensified with great success if a light weight of one design is mixed with the heavy weight of the other.

ITC Souvenir's friendliness is almost equally extended to serif typestyles. Typefaces that have well-defined serifs,

those with a vertical, or nearly vertical weight stress, or typefaces with calligraphic overtones all mix with ITC Souvenir, providing generally excellent results. Imagine ITC Souvenir mixed with Meridien, Trump Mediaeval, Bodoni, or even ITC Zapf Chancery! ITC Souvenir can be the text typeface that is contrasted, or it can serve as a strong display counterpoint to a different text face.

Finally, the old and well-founded rule of designing in family applies exceptionally well to ITC Souvenir. Its four weights of roman and italic designs—plus small caps in the light roman—create a versatile and flexible typographic tool. Producing a long or complicated document in the ITC Souvenir family is a ready solution to good graphics. ITC Souvenir, especially in the medium or bolder weights, possesses the strength to stand up to the problems of reversing type or printing in light colors.

While it allows reasonable degrees of latitude when it comes to letterspacing, ITC Souvenir (because of its large-x-height and open counters) should normally be set with the "tightness switch" in the "off" or "just barely on" position. Setting ITC Souvenir too tight disrupts a naturally even color that benefits design.

Many people use ITC Souvenir, and a lot of particularly good graphics have been set in the design. It can be used within normal parameters with almost absolute assurance of positive results, and it can provide the foundation for some exceptionally creative and innovative graphic communication. Some nice guys do finish first.

Times Roman

ABCDEFGHIJKLMNOPQRSTUVWXYZ
abcdefghijklmnopqrstuvwxyz
1234567890
$)] - ; / — , . ! ([& - : / ? , . ¢ ¿ ¡ ß £/— „ ·

ABCDEFGHIJKLMNOPQRSTUVWXYZ
abcdefghijklmnopqrstuvwxyz
1234567890
$)] - ; / — , . ! ([& - : / ? , . ¢ ¿ ¡ ß £/— „ ·

Times Roman
Times Italic
Times Semi Bold
Times Semi Bold Italic
Times Bold
Times Bold Italic

The type designer is the person given credit for a particular typeface design. Albert Boton is credited with the design of ITC Elan, as is Adrian Frutiger for Univers, and Hermann Zapf for Palatino. Even when the end product is a collaboration of a type designer and a design director, the designer still normally receives most of the credit. As an example, William Dwiggins worked very closely with C. H. Griffith, who was responsible for typographic development at Mergenthaler Linotype early in this century; yet only Dwiggins is always associated with their typeface designs.

Times Roman is an exception. In fact, for a typeface as well known and as much used as Times Roman, there is an inordinate amount of confusion about its origin. Most people believe that Stanley Morison designed the typeface. He did not. He had a major part in the development of the design; it was certainly his idea, his concept. But it was not Stanley Morison who actually rendered the type. An artist, Victor Lardent, working in *The Times* of London art department, actually drew Times Roman.

Another area of confusion is this typeface's name. As released by the British Monotype Corporation, it is known as Times New Roman. Linotype calls the typeface simply Times Roman. *The Times* refers to the face as The Times New Roman. Each is a correct name. Each company owns rights in the design, and each has chosen to call the typeface something different. Regardless of this confusion over its name, Times Roman is one of the most used and most important typefaces in the designer's typographic toolbox.

Attributes

Times Roman is classified as a Dutch Old Style design. Some Dutch Old Style typefaces currently available, such as Plantin, Caslon, and Janson, are revivals of designs actually used in the Netherlands during the seventeenth and eighteenth centuries, but Times Roman was a new design when first released in the early 1930s. Its design traits are its link with the past—not its heritage.

Times Roman varies from the Dutch Old Style norm in a number of distinct ways. Immediately noticeable is the weight contrast; it is more pronounced than most other Old Styles. The weight stress is also carried quite low—to the degree that the lowercase *o* almost appears to tilt backward. Although pronounced, weight transition from thick to thin is not abrupt; this and Times Roman's large x-height make for easy reading in numerous applications and under a variety of conditions. Character proportions are condensed, further increasing its range of applications. Head serifs are angled and, even though bracketed, are only slightly heavier than the foot serifs.

Background

Times Roman was Stanley Morison's idea. In 1929, Morison, already typographic advisor to Monotype, was made typographic advisor to *The Times*. One of his first responsibilities in that position was to redesign the newspaper. As far as Morison was concerned, one of the first tasks in that process was to change the typeface that *The Times* normally used for text composition.

Several existing typestyles were tried first; but Morison and *The Times* executive staff found them unsuitable for one reason or another. These were not arbitrary decisions; *The Times* had a long tradition of providing the news to Londoners in not only exceptional journalistic style but also exemplary typographic style. Since no existing typeface would do, Morison and *The Times* executive staff decided to establish design criteria for creating a totally new design.

The criteria were basically simple: The new design would have to appear larger than its predecessor; it could take up no more space than the existing typeface; it should be heavier than the existing design; it must be highly legible; it must be beautiful.

Morison felt that basing the new design on Plantin would begin to satisfy many of the established criteria. Plantin, being a Dutch Old Style typeface, already had an ample x-height, it was somewhat condensed, and its color was slightly heavier than normal. Many subtle, and a few not so subtle, changes were required, but its design foundation certainly fulfilled the requirements.

Morison provided Victor Lardent with photographs of Plantin specimens and a list of instructions. Thus, the design program was begun, with Morison acting as creative director and Lardent as illustrator/designer. The completed typeface, which was arrived at after a lengthy design process and many revisions, certainly bears a resemblance to Plantin but is also obviously its own design. Serifs had been sharpened from Plantin's, stroke width contrast was increased, and character curves were refined. As a result, Times Roman is considered a more graceful and elegant design than Plantin.

Though Morison believed he was basing his Times on the work of the Dutch printer and type designer, Christopher Plantin, it probably was based on the work of Robert Granjon. Even the typefaces we currently refer to as "Plantin designs" are based on Granjon's fonts (see the chapter on Plantin, above).

Times Roman was first used to print *The Times* in October 1932. One year later, Linotype and Monotype were allowed to offer the family to the typographic community. Although its popularity is renowned today, Times Roman was not an instant worldwide success. It took almost twenty years before it was used to any great extent in America. Today, it is probably used and duplicated on a variety of type-imaging devices more than any other typeface—even more than Helvetica. The Times Roman typestyle is currently available on typewriters, dry-transfer lettering sheets, laser printers, video "screen" fonts, dot-matrix printers, daisy wheels, and virtually every kind of graphic arts composition equipment.

Times Roman

CONSIDERATIONS FOR USE

Times Roman is a workhorse; it can be used for just about any typographic application imaginable. It is an exceptionally legible design and is suitable for a wide variety of printing surfaces. One of Stanley Morison's complaints with the typographic industry was typefaces that too obviously reflected the designer's hand or those that had an overly strong stylistic quality. As a result, Times is not a typeface with a pronounced personality. It does not, of itself, create a mood or feeling. It has but one job—to communicate; it does that exceptionally well.

One of the virtues of a typeface that lacks a distinct personality or stylistic appearance is that it is easy to use with other typefaces. Times Roman is a good mixer. It can be combined with almost any sans serif type design and a great many serif typestyles with no aesthetic conflict. Helvetica is a perfect, if traditional, complement to Times Roman. Other excellent choices from the sans serif category are Antique Olive, Frutiger, and ITC Avant Garde Gothic. The only caution is that the lighter weights of these, or any other sans serif for that matter, should be avoided. Times Roman has a robust color that could easily overpower many lightweight sans serifs.

As far as serif typestyles are concerned, Times Roman will mix well with almost all, except those that have similar design traits. Faces like Plantin, Janson, Caslon, and, to some degree, Baskerville should be avoided. Typefaces that are stylistically in sharp contrast to Times Roman are the best choices. The soft contours and less-formal shapes found in ITC Souvenir, Stempel Schneidler, or Goudy Old Style are natural contrasts to the order and structure of Times Roman. Typefaces with strong, heavy serifs are also worth considering. These could be faces like ITC Lubalin Graph and Rockwell, which have square serifs; or faces like Melior and ITC Cheltenham, which have heavy bracketing. Experiment with the typefaces you mix with Times Roman. You almost cannot go wrong, and the results can be very rewarding.

The ascenders and decenders of Times

This ad is one of several created for Yamaha instruments 1985–86 print ad campaign by Ivan Horvath, vice president/creative director at NW Ayer, Inc., Los Angeles. Times Roman was selected exclusively for the headlines and typeset on Berthold equipment by Andresen Typographics.

Roman are short. In most typographic applications, this causes no problems; in some instances, these proportions can even be considered a benefit. Too much line space, however, can accentuate this design trait and could make the ascenders and descenders appear squat. Times Roman allows for a reasonable amount of line-space adjustment, but not as much as designs like Baskerville or Caledonia, which have proportionately longer ascenders and descenders.

Current typographic trends tend to call for text typefaces that are on the light side. The book weights of large type families have become the most popular. Times Roman has no book weight. It is, in fact, a rather heavy face in the roman. Obviously this has not hurt its popularity; but care should be taken that text set in Times Roman is not made to appear darker than it already is. Letterspacing should be normal. Tight letterspacing will intensify the copy's color and can even create black spots where characters come too close to each other or touch. Margins should be generous, and rules, if used, should be light in weight.

Although some manufacturers do offer semibold and condensed designs of Times Roman, most typesetters have only the basic roman and bold weights—with corresponding italics. Practically speaking, Times Roman is a bit limited. It is an excellent choice for lengthy text composition, and perfectly adequate for all but the most complicated applications; but Times Roman can benefit from the support of other typefaces.

Its condensed proportions and large x-height allow Times Roman to be used where other typefaces would be unacceptable, for instance, in directories and parts lists. But marked weight contrast and fine hairlines make its use inadvisable in most applications below 8 point.

Times Roman has earned its stature in the typographic spectrum. It is versatile, it is legible, and it is an excellent communicator. And, even more—something that is often overlooked about this design—Times Roman is also beautiful.

Another of NW Ayer's Yamaha ads leans heavily toward an all-type design, mixing a Times Roman headline with Original Century body copy.

Univers

ABCDEFGHIJKLMNOPQRSTUVWXYZ
abcdefghijklmnopqrstuvwxyz
1234567890
$)] - ; / — , . ! ([& - : / ? , . ¢ ¿ ¡ ß £/— „ ·

ABCDEFGHIJKLMNOPQRSTUVWXYZ
abcdefghijklmnopqrstuvwxyz
1234567890
$)] - ; / — , . ! ([& - : / ? , . ¢ ¿ ¡ ß £/— „ ·

Univers 45 Light
Univers 46 Light Italic
Univers 55
Univers 56 Italic
Univers 65 Bold
Univers 66 Bold Italic
Univers 75 Black
Univers 76 Black Italic
Univers 47 Light Condensed

Univers is one of the most important typefaces to be released within the past thirty years. It is one of the few type families developed for both metal and phototypesetting technologies, one of the first families to be designed as a cohesive unit prior to release, and finally, it is probably the first typeface family developed for universal licensing.

Univers was produced by the Deberny and Peignot typefoundry at a time when it was still actively selling metal type and had just begun to market one of the first practical phototypesetting devices. Clear thinking and an eye to the future dictated that Univers would have to be made available for both technologies in order to be commercially successful.

An important aspect of the Univers family of type is its modularity. Designer Adrian Frutiger wanted to create a series of related designs that were absolutely harmonious with each other. This could only be accomplished by determining the complete family range as part of the design process or by building the family within a strict modular framework. Frutiger did both.

Seeing diverse business, financial, and ethical reasons for the unlimited licensing of typefaces, Charles Peignot, then the owner and managing director of Deberny and Peignot, chose to license the rights to the design and the name to virtually every supplier of type and text composition equipment. As a result, such diverse companies as Compugraphic Corporation, IBM, and Monotype have licensing agreements for the Univers family. In fact, just about any company that sells type also licenses Univers.

All these positive traits have made it an exceptionally popular typeface in Europe (in some countries even more popular than Helvetica) but, unfortunately, not in the United States.

ATTRIBUTES

Univers can easily be confused with Helvetica; their basic designs are quite similar. But it does not take much study or typographic sophistication to distinguish one design from the other.

Generally, Univers is not as monotone in appearance as Helvetica. (It has more contrast between stroke thicknesses.) This is a design trait that works in favor of Univers. It is generally accepted (and, in fact, proven in a number of studies) that typefaces with a certain amount of obvious stroke contrast are more inviting and are easier to read in lengthy blocks of text copy than typefaces that appear monotone in weight.

Univers also has a slight squaring to its round strokes. They tend to appear flattened when compared to Helvetica. Although this trait is apparent throughout the family, it is most noticeable in the condensed variants. Probably no real typographic benefits are gained from this aspect of Univers's design, but it does provide a certain Gallic panache to the family.

The Univers family is large. Offering twenty-one variants, it is almost as large as the Helvetica family. It is not as varied as Helvetica, however, though it should be more usable because it was more carefully conceived. Helvetica grew "like Topsy." New weights and design variants were added over many years and were developed by several different typeface designers. The result is a large, but not particularly well-integrated type family. This situation has now been corrected in a type family called Neue Helvetica, which was developed within a united design philosophy, as was Univers; but Neue Helvetica has not attained the availability or popularity in the United States either of its parent design or of Univers.

In addition to several broad design traits, a number of individual characters help to distinguish Univers from other designs. One of the more obvious is the lowercase *a*. Similar to Helvetica and many other sans serif designs, the Univers *a* is a two-storied design and looks pretty much like every other two-storied sans serif *a*—until you examine it a little closer. In Univers, this character has a very straight back with almost no baseline curl. In addition, the top of the bowl connects with the main stem at an angle of almost 90 degrees.

The capital and lowercase *k* are also distinguishing letters. The intersections of the diagonals join at the exact point where they meet the vertical stroke. (Generally, the bottom diagonal joins the upper one along that stroke.)

Another letter to look at is the capital *G*. It has a long vertical stem and does not have the spur found on the same letter in Helvetica, ITC Franklin Gothic, or similar alphabets.

The ampersand in Univers is also quite distinctive—at least in many manufacturers' versions of the family. Univers has the European *et* style of ampersand while most other popular sans serif typestyles have the more traditional figure-eight design. Unfortunately, not every manufacturer offers the original Univers design. Several replaced it with the more conventional style of ampersand because they felt that the European version was somewhat alien to American tastes.

BACKGROUND

Adrian Frutiger was a comparatively young man when he drew Univers. It was one of his first designs for the long-established Deberny and Peignot typefoundry.

Charles Peignot was the third generation of his family to manage and oversee the typographic direction of the typefoundry. Being a man of vision, he saw both the threats and the opportunities that phototypesetting and dry-transfer lettering posed for his traditional business. His resulting business plan called for the development and marketing of products to compete in the new typographic environment. Typophane became Deberny and Peignot's dry-transfer product. Lumitype became their phototypesetter. Although neither of these products became household words in the United States, Lumitype was sold in America under the name Photon.

Increasingly, Peignot turned his attention to the Lumitype typeface library, which meant faces not just for the French

Univers

market but for the world. Peignot's remarkable foresight prompted him, after seeing Adrian Frutiger's work in 1952, to convince the young Swiss designer to come to Paris and work for Deberny and Peignot.

When Peignot decided to add a sans serif range to the Lumitype library, he called on Adrian Frutiger. Rather than start from scratch, however, Frutiger persuaded Peignot to allow him to further develop a design concept he had begun in design school. Univers was the result. It was released in the same year as Helvetica, 1957.

In many ways a revolutionary design,

Univers was produced with a then unique system of weight and proportion organization. Since Frutiger felt that the traditional system of providing names (bold, semibold, semibold condensed, and so on) was confusing and outdated, he proposed what he felt was a logical and systematic number scheme. In Frutiger's system, each typeface was given a two-digit suffix. The first digit classified the alphabet weight, the figure 3 indicating the lightest weights in the family and the figure 8 the boldest; the figures 4 and 7 were used for the intermediate weights. The second digit identified the typeface proportion—higher numbers

for condensed designs and lower numbers for expanded designs. In addition, if the second number was odd, the typeface was a roman design; and if it was even, the typeface was italic. Thus, Univers 39 is a very light condensed roman design, Univers 56 is a medium-weight italic of normal proportions, and Univers 83 is a very bold extended roman design. It sounds a little confusing, but actually the system works quite well. Frutiger continued to use this system for all the succeeding typeface designs he created. Unfortunately, few other type designers adopted Frutiger's system, so it stands relatively alone, more of an oddity than

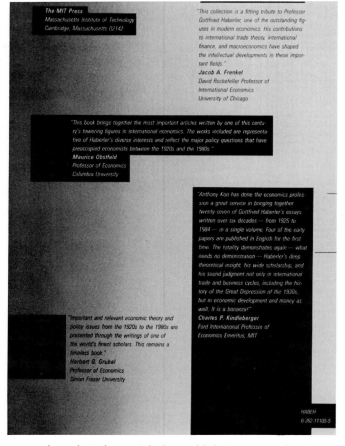

At MIT Press, designers often use sans serif faces for display and text type on the technical materials they publish. Designer Julie Simms, who designed both of the book jackets shown here (one front and one back view), says she prefers the "cut" of Univers over that of Helvetica. "I appreciate the range of weights and styles within Univers. It can be very bold or convey elegance," she says.

the universal tool it was intended to be. In fact, many font suppliers have chosen to convert Frutiger's numbers back to traditional names, for what they believe is the convenience of their customers.

Even though they tampered with the Univers family identification system, font suppliers generally left the alphabet design the way Frutiger intended it. The result is that the graphic communicator can be assured of consistent quality from virtually any supplier.

CONSIDERATIONS FOR USE

Univers is an exceptional typeface for text composition (especially when considering that it is a serifless typeface). It is highly legible, quite inviting when lighter weights are used, and can be surprisingly readable—not a bad choice for many applications.

Because Univers is, after all, a sans serif design, a few typographic details do need attending to. Univers has a naturally even (but not indestructible) typographic color. If letterspacing is set too tight or word spacing too open, Univers can lose much of its appeal and communication power. Therefore, at least for text composition in Univers, it is best not to get too creative with letterspacing or to allow word spacing to get too sloppy.

The lighter weights (45, 55) of Univers are the best choices for text copy. In all but the very smallest sizes, Univers 45 works remarkably well. Its color is surprisingly even for a light typeface, and it is quite easy to read in long blocks of copy. Using the 45 series really has only two drawbacks: At anything below 9 point, it becomes too light for extensive use, and Univers 55 (the next available weight) is not quite bold enough to serve as a good lighter design emphasizer.

Univers 55, which is about the weight and color of Helvetica, is actually the design intended for text copy. It will perform well at virtually all point sizes, and its bold complement (Univers 65) has just the right degree of robustness. Univers 55 should really be considered the default typeface but its lighter cousin

(Univers 45) is more elegant and inviting for many applications.

Many graphic-design projects, such as annual reports, directories, parts lists, magazines, and technical documentation (pieces that are easy to make dull and can lack in continuity), can benefit from the use of several typefaces to aid the reader in the communication process. The Univers family is perfect for these kinds of graphic challenges. It is sufficiently large and diverse to handle practically any communication or design problem. Univers also has a strong family identity that can serve as the thread of continuity binding complicated and lengthy graphics into a dynamic and easy-to-understand unit.

An added benefit from the Univers design is that there is personality and character under its modular exterior. Think of it as a Swiss design with a French heart. As its weight increases, this personality becomes more apparent. The slight (but clearly visible) contrast in stroke weight, subtle angularity, and just the smallest hint of calligraphic brush stroke make Univers a typeface with a twinkle in its eye.

Headlines set in Univers, especially the heavier weights, look different— even to the casual reader. They stand out just a little bit more than headlines set in Helvetica or ITC Franklin Gothic. It may be difficult for the reader to describe this difference, but the character and personality of Univers will surely be felt.

The Univers family contains an exceptional collection of condensed typefaces—more than nine different variants. Not only does Univers offer a wide variety of condensed designs from which to choose, but they are all highly legible without suffering aesthetically. This makes Univers a natural choice for applications in which space is at a premium. Directories, photo captions, timetables, and catalogs all fall within its area of expertise.

Univers is also a good mixer, primarily with serif typestyles and especially with those designed by Frutiger. There is an obvious, but not overpowering, family

resemblance among all of his designs. Serifa, Icone, and Meridian, just to name a few, all combine remarkably well with Univers.

This family should not be restricted, however, to just being mixed with other Frutiger typefaces. Old Styles like ITC Garamond, Kennerly, or Bauer Text will contrast nicely with the crisp angularity and modular uniformity of Univers. The elegance of transitionals like Caledonia and ITC New Baskerville is emphasized when set in conjunction with Univers; their thick and thin stroke contrast and delicate weight transitions seem to take on more rhythm and importance. The British conservatism of Times Roman counterplays beautifully with Univers's Gallic spark. To some extent, Univers is like a fine wine that augments and adds slight complexity to a meal.

Mixing Univers with other sans serifs, however, is a little like mixing that fine wine with carbonated soda—neither benefits from the combination. Generally, sans serif typefaces do not mix well with each other; Univers mixes more poorly than most, being basically similar in design to other sans serifs.

Since typography has no absolute rules, there are situations and circumstances in which Univers might be mixed with another sans serif design with admirable results. Try it with Antique Olive (especially if contrasting weights are used), with ITC Avant Garde Gothic, or with Gill Sans. Striking graphics can result if the typography is handled with care.

There is one important drawback to using Univers. It is not used much in the United States, and the full family (sometimes even parts of it) is not readily available from most type houses. If you can find a type supplier who offers the full range of the Univers family, it can be put to use creating graphics that stand out from the crowd.

Like many things French, Univers has rare beauty, charm, and a distinct personality. Like many things rare, it must be searched for. Univers is well worth the search.

TYPEFACE ANALOGUE

INTRODUCTION TO THE TYPEFACE ANALOGUE

In his original preface to the "Typeface Analogue," William Wheatley wrote:

This is an update to the original edition of the Typeface Analogue released in 1985. Many additions have been made to this latest edition, including more of the "desktop publishing" names which are getting used, as well as all the names of some of the new typefaces being manufactured by different companies.

The analogue was put together to enable typeface specifiers and typographers, as well as interested individuals, to identify typefaces by the names given them by different manufacturers. I have tried to include all typefaces which have more than one name, and have cross-referenced them for easy identification.

I have included as many sources as possible, and have included office equipment manufacturers as well as type foundries and typesetting manufacturers.

In compiling this type of list there is always chance for error, and although I have checked my sources carefully, I may have missed something through an oversight. If anyone discovers any correction or alteration, please let me know. Also, if anyone knows of any typeface I may have missed, I would like to know that to add to a future edition of this publication.*

Typeface designs have been plagued by the confusion of multiple names practically since Gutenberg's time. Early on, this was not too much of a problem for graphic communicators—simply because there were not very many faces available. As the typographic palette increased in size, however, so did the problem. Various attempts were made to cross reference the numerous names to similar typestyles, but none were particularly successful.

In the mid-1970s AGFA Compugraphic undertook the task of creating a useful, accurate, and reasonably definitive typeface analogue. Over the past several years this basic cross-reference guide has been updated and reprinted several times. The current curator of this resource is William Wheatley, a man who has held a variety of marketing and production jobs in the typographic industry. The "Typeface Analogue" in this book is an updated, and somewhat simplified, version of William Wheatley's work.

This version does not include typefaces that do not have at least one similar design by a different name. So faces like Bitstream Charter, ITC Benguiat, or Adobe's Utopia are not listed because they are available from suppliers only under those names. In addition, this analogue does not include companies that offer typefaces under license agreements from the originating founder. For example: since Adobe licenses Monotype's Gill Sans there is no listing for Adobe under Gill Sans.

Some typefaces that are no longer available may not be listed, and an asterisked typefoundry name indicates that the originating foundry may no longer be in business.

Manufacturers' Names

The manufacturers names used (in alphabetical order):

Adobe Systems
Electronic typefoundry
Mountain View, California

Alphatype Corp.
Typesetter manufacturer
Niles, Illinois

Am International Inc.
Typesetter manufacturer
East Hanover, New Jersey

American Type Founders
Typefoundry*
Elizabeth, New Jersey
(bought the other US Foundries)

Apple Computer, Inc.
Computer manufacturer
Cupertino, California

Autologic, Inc.
Typesetter manufacturer
Newbury Park, California

Baltimore Type Foundry
Typefoundry*
Baltimore, Maryland

Bauersche Giesserie (Bauer)
Typefoundry*
Frankfurt, West Germany
(now Neufville, S.A., Spain)

H. Berthold AG
Typesetter manufacturer
Berlin, West Germany

Bitstream, Inc.
Electronic typefoundry
Cambridge, Massachusetts

H.W. Caslon
Typefoundry*
England
(bought by Stephenson Blake in 1937)

AGFA Compugraphic
Typesetter manufacturer
Wilmington, Massachusetts

Dearborn Foundry
Typefoundry*
Chicago, Illinois
(bought by American Type Founders)

Deberney & Peignot
Typefoundry*
Paris, France

Haas'sche Schriftgiesserei AG
Typefoundry
Munchenstein, Switzerland

Information International, Inc. (III)
Typesetter manufacturer
Culver City, California

Inland Type Foundry*
Chicago, Illinois
(bought by American Type Founders)

**International Business
Machines Corp. (IBM)**
Computer manufacturer
Armonk, New York

Intertype Company
Typesetter manufacturer*
Brooklyn, New York
(now Harris Composition Systems)

Itek Composition Systems
Typesetter manufacturer
Nashua, New Hampshire

Lanston Monotype Co.
Typesetter manufacturer*
Philadelphia, Pennsylvania
(now combined with Monotype
Corp., UK)

Letraset Ltd.
Transfer lettering sheet manufacturer
London, England

Linotype AG
Typesetter manufacturer
Hauppauge, New York
(now Linotype AG)

Ludlow Typography Company
Typesetter manufacturer*
Chicago, Illinois

Ludwig & Mayer GmbH
Typefoundry*
Frankfurt, West Germany

Monotype Corporation Ltd.
Typesetter manufacturer
Salfords Redhill, England

Societa Nebiolo
Typefoundry*
Turin, Italy

Fundicion Tipografica Neufville, S.A.
Typefoundry*
Barcelona, Spain (see Bauer)

Quality Micro Systems, Inc. (QMS)
Laser printer manufacturer
Mobile, Alabama

Scangraphic Dr. Boger GmbH
Typesetter manufacturer
Wedel/Hamburg, West Germany

D. Stempel AG
Typefoundry*
Frankfurt am Main, West Germany

Stephenson Blake & Co. Ltd.
Typefoundry*
Sheffield, England

Visual Graphics Corporation
Headline machine manufacturer
Tamarac, Florida

J. Wagner
Typefoundry*
Ingolstadt, Donau, East Germany

C.E. Weber
Typefoundry*
Stuttgart, West Germany

A. Williams Design Limited
Type designer
Sutton, Surrey, England

Xerox Corporation
Printer manufacturer
El Segundo, California

TYPEFACE LISTING

A

Aachen (Letraset)
Charlemagne (Tegra)
Ruhr (III)

Abbey (Autologic)
Cloister Text (ATF)
Goudy Text (Lan. Mon.)

Ace (Itek)
University Roman (Letraset)

Ad Bold (Photon)
Brush Roman (III)
Dom Casual (ATF)
Polka (Berthold)

Ad Gothic (Autologic)
Ad Sans (Lino)
News Ad (Harris)

Ad Grotesk (Scangraphic)
Standard (Berthold)

Airport (Baltimore)
Alphatura (Alphatype)
Futura (Bauer)
Future (Alphatype)
Geometric 212 (Bitstream)
Sparta (Autologic)
Spartan (Lino)
Technica (III)
Twentieth Century (Monotype)

Aldine 401 (Bitstream)
Aldine Roman (IBM)
Bem (CG)
Bembo (Monotype)
Griffo (Alphatype)

Aldine Roman (IBM)
Aldine 401 (Bitstream)
Bem (CG)
Bembo (Monotype)
Griffo (Alphatype)

Aldostyle (Autologic)
Eurogothic (Alphatype)
Eurostile (Nebiolo)
Eurostyle (CG)
Gamma (III)
Microgramma (Nebiolo)
Microstyle (CG)
Square 721 (Bitstream)

Alexandria

Beton (Neufville)
Geometric slabserif 703 (Bitstream)
Memphis (Stempel)
CG Nashville (CG)
Pyramid (IBM)
Rockwell (Monotype)
Stymie (ATF)

Alpha Gothic (Alphatype)
Classified News (IBM)
News Gothic (ATF)
CG Trade (CG)
Trade Gothic (Lino)

Alphatura (Alphatype)
Airport (Baltimore)
Futura (Bauer)
Future (Alphatype)
Geometric 212 (Bitstream)
Sparta (Autologic)
Spartan (Lino)
Technica (III)
Twentieth Century (Monotype)

Alphavers (Alphatype)
Eterna (III)
Kosmos (Xerox)
CG Univers (CG)
Univers (D&P)
Versatile (Alphatype)
Zurich (Bitstream)

Alpin Gothic (CG)
Alternate Gothic (ATF)

Alternate Gothic (ATF)
Alpin Gothic (CG)

Alphavanti (Alphatype)
Antique Olive (Olive)
Berry Roman (III)
Incised 901 (Bitstream)
Oliva (Autologic)
Olive (Tegra)

Americana (ATF)
American Classic (CG)
Colonial (Tegra)
Concord (III)
Freedom (Autologic)
Independence (Alphatype)

American Classic (CG)
Americana (ATF)
Colonial (Tegra)
Concord (III)

Freedom (Autologic)
Independence (Alphatype)

Antique Olive (Olive)
Alphavanti (Alphatype)
Berry Roman (III)
Incised 901 (Bitstream)
Oliva (Autologic)
Olive (Tegra)

Antique Open (Lino)
Roman Stylus (CG)
Typo Roman Open (ATF)

Antique Solid (Lino)
Typo Roman (ATF)

Anzeigen Grotesk (Berthold)
Aura (CG)
Aurora (Alphatype)
Aurora Bold Condensed
Grotesque Condensed (Photon)

Aquarius (CG)
Cardinal (III)
Corona (Lino)
Crown (Photon)
Koronna (Alphatype)
News No. 3 (CG)
News No. 5 (CG)
News No. 6 (CG)
News 705 (Bitstream)
Nimbus (Alphatype)
Royal (Intertype)

Aristocrat (Tegra)
Akzidenz-Grotesk Buch (Berthold)
Claro (Alphatype)
Europa Grotesk (Scangraphic)
Geneva (Autologic)
Hamilton (QMS)
Helios (CG)
Helvetica (Lino)
Megaron (Tegra)
Newton (Photon)
Sonoran San Serif (IBM)
Spectra (III)
Swiss 721 (Bitstream)
CG Triumvirate (CG)
Vega (Harris)

Ascot (Autologic)
Continental (Harris)
Kuenstler 480 (Bitstream)
Mediaeval (Tegra)

Olympus (Alphatype)
Rennaissance (III)
Saul (Autologic)
CG Trump Mediaeval (CG)
Trump Mediaeval (Weber)

Aster (Nebiolo)
Astro (Alphatype)
Aztec (Autologic)
Corolla (Harris)
Dutch 823 (Bitstream)

Astro (Alphatype)
Aster (Nebiolo)
Aztec (Autologic)
Corolla (Harris)
Dutch 823 (Bitstream)

Atalante (Nebiolo)
Copperplate
Copperplate Gothic (ATF)
Formal Gothic (Photon)
Lining Plate Gothic (Ludlow)
Mimosa (Typoart)
Plate Gothic (Weber)
Spartan (Monotype)

Athena (Autologic)
Musica (Alphatype)
October (Scangraphic)
CG Omega (CG)
Optima (Lino)
Optimist (Autologic)
Oracle (CG)
Roma (III)
Theme (IBM)
Zapf Humanist 601 (Bitstream)

Atlantic (Alphatype)
Plantin (CG)

Aura (CG)
Anzeigen Grotesk (Berthold)
Aurora (Alphatype)
Aurora Bold Condensed
Grotesque Condensed (Photon)

Auriga (Lino)
Riga (Autologic)

Aurora (Lino)
News No. 2 (CG)
News No. 12 (CG)

Aurora (Alphatype)
Aura (CG)

Anzeigen Grotesk (Berthold)
Aurora Bold Condensed
Grotesque Condensed (Photon)

Aurora Bold Condensed
Aurora (Alphatype)
Aura (CG)
Anzeigen Grotesk (Berthold)

Avanta (III)
Elante (CG)
Electra (Lino)
Illumna (Harris)
Selectra (Autologic)
Transitional 321 (Bitstream)

Aztec (Autologic)
Aster (Nebiolo)
Astro (Alphatype)
Corolla (Harris)
Dutch 823 (Bitstream)

B

Balloon (ATF)
Kaufman (Tegra)
Kaufman Script (ATF)
L.A. Script (Autologic)
Swing Bold (Monotype)
Tropez (CG)

Bank Gothic (ATF)
Bankers Gothic
Magnum Gothic (CG)

Bankers Gothic
Bank Gothic (ATF)
Magnum Gothic (CG)
Stationer's Gothic (Lan. Mono.)

Baskerline (Alphatype)
Baskerville

Baskerville
Baskerline (Alphatype)

Basque (Lino)
Vascones Text (Autologic)

Bauen Schrift (Autologic)
Bauer Text (Neufville)
Brewer Text (Alphatype)

Bauer Text (Neufville)
Bauen Schrift (Autologic)
Brewer Text (Alphatype)

Bell Gothic (Lino)
Directory Gothic (CG)

Bern (CG)
Aldine 401 (Bitstream)
Aldine Roman (IBM)
Bembo (Monotype)
Griffo (Alphatype)

Bembo (Monotype)
Aldine 401 (Bitstream)
Aldine Roman (IBM)
Bem (CG)
Griffo (Alphatype)

Berlin (Harris)
Camelot (Tegra)
Esquire (Scangraphic)
Excel (Autologic)
Excelsior (Lino)
League Text (Alphatype)
News No. 9 (CG)
News No. 14 (CG)

Berner (Tegra)
Classical Garamond (Bitstream)
Sabon
September (Scangraphic)
Sybil (Autologic)

Berry Roman (III)
Alphavanti (Alphatype)
Antique Olive (Olive)
Incised 901 (Bitstream)
Oliva (Autologic)
Olive (Tegra)

Beton (Neufville)
Memphis (Stempel)
CG Nashville (CG)
Pyramid (IBM)
Rockwell (Monotype)
Stymie (ATF)

Boston Script (Alphatype)
Embassy Script (Caslon)
Formal Script (Ludlow)
Helanna Script (Tegra)
Lucia Script (Lino)
Original Script (CG)
Typo Script (ATF)
Yorkshire Script (Alphatype)

Boulevard (Berthold)
Francine (Tegra)

Brewer Text (Alphatype)

Bauer Text (Neufville)

Bridal Text (Alphatype)
Nuptial Script (Harris)

Brody (ATF)
Brophy Script (CG)

Brophy Script (CG)
Brody (ATF)

Brunswick (Tegra)
Poppl-Pontifex (Berthold)
Power (Scangraphic)

Brush Roman (III)
Ad Bold (Photon)
Dom Casual (ATF)
Polka (Berthold)

C

Calderon (Scangraphic)
Caledo (Alphatype)
Caledonia (Lino)
CG California (CG)
Gael (III)
Highland (Tegra)

Caledo (Alphatype)
Calderon (Scangraphic)
Caledonia (Lino)
CG California (CG)
Gael (III)
Highland (Tegra)

Caledonia (Lino)
Calderon (Scangraphic)
Caledo (Alphatype)
CG California (CG)
Gael (III)
Highland (Tegra)

CG California (CG)
Calderon (Scangraphic)
Caledo (Alphatype)
Caledonia (Lino)
Gael (III)
Highland (Tegra)

Camelot (Tegra)
Berlin (Harris)
Esquire (Scangraphic)
Excel (Autologic)
Excelsior (Lino)
League Text (Alphatype)

News No. 9 (CG)
News No. 14 (CG)

Candida (Ludwig & Mayer)
Antique 505 (J. Wagner)
Candide (Alphatype)

Candide (Alphatype)
Antique 505 (J. Wagner)
Candida (Ludwig & Meyer)

Cardinal (III)
Aquarius (CG)
Corona (Lino)
Crown (Photon)
Koronna (Alphatype)
News No. 3 (CG)
News No. 5 (CG)
News No. 6 (CG)
Nimbus (Alphatype)
Royal (Intertype)

Carmine Tango (CG)
Bernhard Tango (ATF)

Cascade Script (Lino)
Kaskade Script (Autologic)

Catalina (Autologic)
Waverly (Intertype)

Centaur (Monotype)
Centaurus (Alphatype)
Classic Text (Itek)

Centaurus (Alphatype)
Centaur (Monotype)
Classic Text (Itek)

Century Expanded (ATF)
Century Light (CG)
Century Oldstyle
Century X (Alphatype)

Century Light (CG)
Century Expanded (ATF)
Century Oldstyle
Century X (Alphatype)

Century Medium (IBM)
Century Modern
Century Schoolbook (ATF)
Century Text (Alphatype)
Century Textbook (CG)
Schoolbook (Tegra)

Century Modern
Century Medium (IBM)

Century Schoolbook (ATF)
Century Text (Alphatype)
Century Textbook (CG)
Schoolbook (Tegra)

Century Nova (ATF)
Manchester Condensed (CG)

Century Schoolbook (ATF)
Century Medium (IBM)
Century Modern
Century Text (Alphatype)
Century Textbook (CG)
Schoolbook (Tegra)

Century Text (Alphatype)
Century Medium (IBM)
Century Modern
Century Schoolbook (ATF)
Century Textbook (CG)
Schoolbook (Tegra)

Century Textbook (CG)
Century Medium (IBM)
Century Modern
Century Schoolbook (ATF)
Century Text (Alphatype)
Schoolbook (Tegra)

Century X (Alphatype)
Century Expanded (ATF)
Century Light (CG)
Century Oldstyle

Chapel Script (Photon)
Mahogany Script (CG)

Charlemagne (Tegra)
Aachen (Letraset)
Ruhr (III)

Chatsworth (Autologic)
Radiant (Ludlow)

Chelmsford (Photon)
Athena (Autologic)
Musica (Alphatype)
October (Scangraphic)
CG Omega (CG)
Optima (Lino)
Optimist (Autologic)
Oracle (CG)
Roma (III)
Theme (IBM)

Chelsea (Photon)
Gothic No. 2 (CG)

Gothic No. 3 (CG)
Meteor (Autologic)
Metro (Lino)
Metromedium (III)

Cheltenham (ATF)
Gloucester (Monotype)
Nordoff (Autologic)
Sorbonne (Berthold)
Winchester (Stephenson-Blake)

Chinchilla (Scangraphic)
Concert (Alphatype)
Concorde (Berthold)
Transport (Tegra)

Cintal (Tegra)
CG Symphony (CG)
Synchron (Scangraphic)
Syntax (Lino)
Synthesis (Autologic)

City (Berthold)
Tower (ATF)
Town (Autologic)

Clarendon
Clarion (Autologic)

Clarion (Autologic)
Clarendon

Clarizo (Autologic)
Egizio (Nebiolo)

Claro (Alphatype)
Europa Grotesk (Scangraphic)
Geneva (Autologic)
Hamilton (QMS)
Helios (CG)
Helvetica (Lino)
Megaron (Tegra)
Sonoran San Serif (IBM)
Spectra (III)
Swiss 721 (Bitstream)
CG Triumvirate (CG)

Classic Text (Itek)
Centaur (Monotype)
Centaurus (Alphatype)

Classical Garamond (Bitstream)
Berner (AM)
Sabon (Lino)
September (Scangraphic)
Sybil (Autologic)

Classified News (IBM)
Alpha Gothic (Alphatype)
News Gothic (ATF)
Record Gothic (Ludlow)
CG Trade (CG)
Trade Gothic (Lino)

Cloister Text (ATF)
Abbey (Autologic)
Goudy Text (Lan. Mono.)

Cochin (Ludwig & Mayer)
Cochine (Autologic)
CG Collage (CG)
Gravure (Amsterdam)
LeCochin (Berthold)
Nicolas Cochin (Lan. Mono.)
Traverse (Tegra)

Cochine (Autologic)
Cochin (Ludwig & Mayer)
CG Collage (CG)
Gravure (Amsterdam)
LeCochin (Berthold)
Nicolas Cochin (Lan. Mono.)
Traverse (Tegra)

CG Collage (CG)
Cochin (Ludwig & Mayer)
Cochine (Autologic)
Gravure (Amsterdam)
LeCochin (Berthold)
Nicolas Cochin (Lan. Mono.)
Traverse (Tegra)

Colonial (Tegra)
Americana (ATF)
American Classic (CG)
Concord (III)
Freedom (Autologic)
Independence (Alphatype)

Computer (CG)
Moore Computer

Command (Autologic)
Mandate (Ludlow)

Compano (III)
Malibu (Autologic)
CG Palacio (CG)
Paladium (CG)
Palatino (Lino)
Parlament (Scangraphic)
Patina (Alphatype)

Concert (Alphatype)
Chinchilla (Scangraphic)
Concorde (Berthold)
Transport (Tegra)

Concord (III)
Colonial (Tegra)
Americana (ATF)
American Classic (CG)
Freedom (Autologic)
Independence (Alphatype)

Concorde (Berthold)
Chinchilla (Scangraphic)
Concert (Alphatype)
Transport (Tegra)

Continental Script (Autologic)
Minuet (Harris)
Piranesi Italic (ATF)

Contessa (Photon)
Loren (III)
Torino (Nebiolo)

Cooper Black (ATF)
Pabst Extra Bold (Lino)
Rugged Black (Harris)

Copperplate Gothic (ATF)
Copperplate
Formal Gothic (Photon)
Lining Plate Gothic (Ludlow)
Spartan (Monotype)

Corinth (Autologic)
Doric (Photon)
Dow News (Photon)
Ideal (Intertype)
Ionic #5 (Lino)
Ionic #342 (Monotype)
News Text (Alphatype)
Regal (Intertype)
Rex (Harris)
Windsor (Harris)
Zar (Photon)

Corolla (Harris)
Aster (Nebiolo)
Astro (Alphatype)
Aztec (Autologic)

Corona (Lino)
Aquarius (CG)
Cardinal (III)
Crown (Photon)

Koronna (Alphatype)
News No. 3 (CG)
News No. 5 (CG)
News No. 6 (CG)
Nimbus (Alphatype)
Royal (Intertype)

Corvina (Autologic)
Corvinus (Bauer)
Eden (Ludlow)
Elegis (Photon)
Glamour (Lan. Mono.)

Corvinus (Bauer)
Corvina (Autologic)
Eden (Ludlow)
Elegis (Photon)
Glamour (Lan. Mono.)

Courier (IBM)
Courrier (Scangraphic)
Messenger (III)
Monaco (Apple)

Courrier (Scangraphic)
Courier (IBM)
Messenger (III)
Monaco (Apple)

Craw Modern (ATF)
Modern (Tegra)

Crown (Photon)
Aquarius (CG)
Cardinal (III)
Corona (Lino)
Koronna (Alphatype)
News No. 3 (CG)
News No. 5 (CG)
News No. 6 (CG)
Nimbus (Alphatype)
Royal (Intertype)

D

Dahlia (CG)
Della Robbia (ATF)

Della Robbia (ATF)
Dahila (CG)

Delmar (Autologic)
Belmont (Photon)
Erbar (Ludwig & Mayer)

Derek Italic (CG)

Doric Black (Lino)
Rhea (Tegra)

Diethelm (Haas)
Patrician (Harris)

Directory Gothic (CG)
Bell Gothic (Lino)

Dom Casual (ATF)
Ad Bold (Photon)
Brush Roman (III)
Polka (Berthold)

Dominae (Autologic)
Dominante (Lino)

Dominante (Lino)
Dominae (Autologic)

Doric Black (Lino)
Derek Italic (CG)
Rhea (Tegra)

Dunkirk (Tegra)
Horley Old Style (Monotype)
Horus Old Style (Autologic)

Durante (Autologic)
Meandme (III)
Umbra (Ludlow)

Dutch 801 (Bitstream)
English (Alphatype)
English 49 (CG)
English Times (CG)
New York (Apple)
Press Roman (IBM)
Sonoran Serif (IBM)
CG Times (CG)
Times New Roman (Monotype)
Times Roman (Lino)
Varitimes (Tegra)

Dutch 809 (Bitstream)
Chinchilla (Scangraphic)
Concert (Alphatype)
Concorde (Berthold)
Transport (AM)

Dutch 823 (Bitstream)
Aster (Nebiolo)
Aztec (Autologic)
Astro (Alphatype)

Dutch Oldstyle (CG)
Janson
Jason (Autologic)

E

Edelweiss (Alphatype)
Weiss (Bauer)

Egizio (Nebiolo)
Clarizo (Autologic)

Egypt 55 (Tegra)
Egyptian 505 (Lino)
Egyptios (Autologic)

Egyptian Bold Condensed
Pharaoh (Autologic)

Egyptian 505 (Lino)
Egypt 55 (Tegra)
Egyptios (Autologic)

Egyptios (Autologic)
Egypt 55 (Tegra)
Egyptian 505 (Lino)

Elante (CG)
Avanta (III)
Electra (Lino)
Selectra (Autologic)

Electra (Lino)
Avanta (III)
Elante (CG)
Selectra (Autologic)

Embassy Script (Caslon)
Boston Script (Alphatype)
Florentine Script (Photon)
Helanna Script (Tegra)
Lucia Script (Lino)
Original Script (CG)
Typo Script (ATF)
Yorkshire Script (Alphatype)

Emperor (III)
Gazette (Lino)
Imperial (Intertype)
New Bedford (Autologic)
News No. 4 (CG)

English (Alphatype)
Dutch 801 (Bitstream)
English 49 (CG)
English Times (CG)
New York (Apple)
Press Roman (IBM)
Sonoran Serif (IBM)
CG Times (CG)
Times New Roman (Monotype)

Times Roman (Lino)
Varitimes (Tegra)

English 49 (CG)
Dutch 801 (Bitstream)
English (Alphatype)
English Times (CG)
New York (Apple)
Press Roman (IBM)
Sonoran Serif (IBM)
CG Times (CG)
Times New Roman (Monotype)
Times Roman (Lino)
Varitimes (Tegra)

English Times (CG)
Dutch 801 (Bitstream)
English 49 (CG)
English (Alphatype)
New York (Apple)
Press Roman (IBM)
CG Times (CG)
Sonoran Serif (IBM)
Times New Roman (Monotype)
Times Roman (Lino)
Varitimes (Tegra)

Engravers Roundhand (Autologic)
Penman Script (Tegra)
Roundhand (Itek)
Roundhand No. 1 (Alphatype)
Signet Roundhand (CG)
Snell Roundhand (Lino)

Equator (Tegra)
Latine (Autologic)
Maximal (CG)
Meridien (D&P)
Meridian (III)

Eric (Alphatype)
Gill Sans (Monotype)
Glib (Alphatype)

Esquire (Scangraphic)
Camelot (Tegra)
Excel (Autologic)
Excelsior (Lino)
League Text (Alphatype)
News No. 9 (CG)
News No. 14 (CG)

Eterna (III)
Alphavers (Alphatype)
Kosmos (Xerox)

CG Univers (CG)
Univers (D&P)
Versatile (Alphatype)

Eurogothic (Alphatype)
Aldostyle (Autologic)
Eurostile (Nebiolo)
Eurostyle (CG)
Gamma (III)
Microgramma (Nebiolo)
Microstyle (CG)

Europa Grotesk (Scangraphic)
Akzidenz-Grotesk Buch (Berthold)
Aristocrat (Tegra)
Claro (Alphatype)
Geneva (Autologic)
Hamilton (QMS)
Helios (CG)
Helvetica (Lino)
Megaron (Tegra)
Sonoran San Serif (IBM)
Spectra (III)
Swiss 721 (Bitstream)
CG Triumvirate (CG)

Europe (D&P)
Airport (Baltimore)
Alphatura (Alphatype)
Contempa (Harris)
Futura (Bauer)
Future (Alphatype)
Sparta (Autologic)
Spartan (Lino)
Technica (III)
Twentieth Century (Monotype)

Eurostile (Nebiolo)
Aldostyle (Autologic)
Eurogothic (Alphatype)
Eurostyle (CG)
Gamma (III)
Microgramma (Nebiolo)
Microstyle (CG)

Eurostyle (CG)
Aldostyle (Autologic)
Eurogothic (Alphatype)
Eurostile (Nebiolo)
Gamma (III)
Microgramma (Nebiolo)
Microstyle (CG)

Excel (Autologic)
Camelot (Tegra)

Esquire (Scangraphic)
Excelsior (Lino)
League Text (Alphatype)
News No. 9 (CG)
News No. 14 (CG)

Excelsior (Lino)
Camelot (Tegra)
Esquire (Scangraphic)
Excel (Autologic)
League Text (Alphatype)
News No. 9 (CG)
News No. 14 (CG)

F

Fairefax (Autologic)
Fairefield (Lino)
Fairmont (Alphatype)

Fairfield (Lino)
Fairefax (Autologic)
Fairmont (Alphatype)

Fairmont (Alphatype)
Fairefax (Autologic)
Fairfield (Lino)
Savant (Harris)

Florentine Script (Photon)
Boston Script (Alphatype)
Embassy Script (Caslon)
Formal Script (Ludlow)
Helanna Script (Tegra)
Imperial Script (Stephenson Blake)
Lucia Script (Lino)
Marina Script (Stephenson Blake)
Original Script (CG)
Palace Script (Stephenson Blake)
Society Script (Stephenson Blake)
Typo Script (ATF)
Yorkshire Script (Alphatype)

Floridian Script (Photon)
Bridal Text (Alphatype)
Nuptial Script (Harris)

Formal Gothic (Photon)
Atalante (Nebiolo)
Copperplate
Copperplate Gothic (ATF)
Lining Plate Gothic (Ludlow)
Mimosa (Typoart)
Plate Gothic (Weber)

Spartan (Monotype)

Formal Script (Ludlow)
Boston Script (Alphatype)
Embassy Script (Caslon)
Florentine Script (Photon)
Helanna Script (Tegra)
Imperial Script (Stephenson Blake)
Lucia Script (Lino)
Marina Script (Stephenson Blake)
Original Script (CG)
Palace Script (Stephenson Blake)
Society Script (Stephenson Blake)
Typo Script (ATF)
Yorkshire Script (Alphatype)

Francine (Tegra)
Boulevard (Berthold)
Francesca (Autologic)

Franklin (CG)
Franklin Gothic (ATF)

Franklin Gothic (ATF)
Franklin (CG)

Frankfurter (Letraset)
Hot Dog (Autologic)

Fredonia (Tegra)
Life (Simoncini)

Freeborn (Scangraphic)
CG Frontiera (CG)
Frutiger (Lino)
Provencale (Autologic)
Siegfried (Tegra)

Freedom (Autologic)
Americana (ATF)
American Classic (CG)
Colonial (Tegra)
Concord (III)
Independence (Alphatype)

French Script (CG)
Kaylin Script (Tegra)
Parisian Ronde (Stephenson Blake)
Typo Upright (ATF)

CG Frontiera (CG)
Freeborn (Scangraphic)
Frutiger (Lino)
Provencale (Autologic)
Siegfried (Tegra)

Frutiger (Lino)

Freeborn (Scangraphic)
CG Frontiera (CG)
Provencale (Autologic)
Siegfried (Tegra)

Futura (Bauer)
Alphatura (Alphatype)
Future (Alphatype)
Sparta (Autologic)
Spartan (Lino)
Technica (III)
Twentieth Century (Monotype)

Future (Alphatype)
Alphatura (Alphatype)
Futura (Bauer)
Sparta (Autologic)
Spartan (Lino)
Technica (III)
Twentieth Century (Monotype)

G

Gael (III)
Calderon (Scangraphic)
Caledo (Alphatype)
Caledonia (Lino)
CG California (CG)
Highland (Tegra)

Gamma (III)
Aldostyle (Autologic)
Eurogothic (Alphatype)
Eurostile (Nebiolo)
Eurostyle (CG)
Microgramma (Nebiolo)
Microstyle (CG)

Garamond (Simoncini)
Garamondus (Autologic)

Garamondus (Autologic)
Garamond (Simoncini)

Garamont Premier (Autologic)
Granjon (Lino)

Garth Graphic (CG)
Matt Antique (Itek)

Gazette (Lino)
Emperor (III)
New Bedford (Autologic)
News No. 4 (CG)

Geneva (Autologic)

Akzidenz-Grotesk Buch (Berthold)
Aristocrat (Tegra)
Claro (Alphatype)
Europa Grotesk (Scangraphic)
Hamilton (QMS)
Helios (CG)
Helvetica (Lino)
Megaron (Tegra)
Sonoran San Serif (IBM)
Spectra (III)
Swiss 721 (Bitstream)
CG Triumvirate (CG)
Vega (Harris)

Genneken (Tegra)
Grotesk-S (Scangraphic)
Neuzeit-Grotesk (Berthold)

Gentlemen (Scangraphic)
Glypha (Lino)

Geometric 212 (Bitstream)
Alphatura (Alphatype)
Airport (Baltimore)
Futura (Bauer)
Futura (Alphatype)
Photura (Photon)
Sparta (Autologic)
Spartan (Lino)
Stylon (Photon)
Technica (III)
Tempo (Ludlow)
Twentieth Century (Monotype)
Vogue (Intertype)

Geometric 415 (Bitstream)
Gothic No. 2 (CG)
Gothic No. 3 (CG)
Meteor (Autologic)
Metro (Lino)
Metromedium (III)

Geometric 706 (Bitstream)
Gennolean (AM)
Grotesk-S (Scangraphic)
Neuzeit-Grotesk (Berthold)

Geometric Slabserif 703 (Bitstream)
Alexandria (Intertype)
Beton (Neufville)
Cairo (Intertype)
Karnak (Ludlow)
Memphis (Stempel)
CG Nashville (CG)
Pyramid (IBM)

Rockwell (Monotype)
Stymie (ATF)

Gill Sans (Monotype)
Eric (Alphatype)
Glib (Alphatype)

Glamour (Lan. Mono.)
Corvina (Autologic)
Corvinus (Bauer)

Glib (Alphatype)
Eric (Alphatype)
Gill Sans (Monotype)

Gloucester (Monotype)
Cheltenham (ATF)
Nordoff (Autologic)
Sorbonne (Berthold)
Winchester (Stephenson-Blake)

Glypha (Lino)
Gentlemen (Scangraphic)

Gold Nugget (CG)
Gold Rush (ATF)
Woop De Doo Bold (Tegra)

Gold Rush (ATF)
Gold Nugget (CG)
Woop De Doo Bold (Tegra)

Gothic No. 1 (CG)
Gothic 19 (Lino)

Gothic No. 2 (CG)
Gothic No. 3 (CG)
Meteor (Autologic)
Metro (Lino)
Metromedium (III)

Gothic No. 3 (CG)
Gothic No. 2 (CG)
Meteor (Autologic)
Metro (Lino)
Metromedium (III)

Gothic No. 4 (CG)
Gothic No. 13 (Lino)

Gothic No. 13 (Lino)
Gothic No. 4 (CG)

Gothic 19 (Lino)
Gothic No. 1 (CG)

Gothic Outline (Tegra)
Gothic Outline Condensed (CG)
Whedon's Gothic Outline (ATF)

Gothic Outline Condensed (CG)
Gothic Outline (Tegra)
Whedon's Gothic Outline (ATF)

Goudy Text (Lan. Mono.)
Abbey (Autologic)
Cloister Text (ATF)

Granjon (Lino)
Garamont Premier (Autologic)

Gravure (Amsterdam)
Cochin (Ludwig & Mayer)
Cochine (Autologic)
CG Collage (CG)
LeCochin (Berthold)
Traverse (Tegra)

Grayda (ATF)
Jasper (CG)

Griffo (Alphatype)
Aldine Roman (IBM)
Bem (CG)
Bembo (Monotype)
Latinesque (Harris)

Grigat (Tegra)
Akzidenz-Grotesk (Berthold)

Grotesk-S (Scangraphic)
Genneken (Tegra)
Neuzeit-Grotesk (Berthold)

H

Hamilton (QMS)
Akzidenz-Grotesk Buch (Berthold)
Aristocrat (Tegra)
Claro (Alphatype)
Europa Grotesk (Scangraphic)
Geneva (Autologic)
Helios (CG)
Helvetica (Lino)
Megaron (Tegra)
Sonoran San Serif (IBM)
Spectra (III)
Swiss 721 (Bitstream)
CG Triumvirate (CG)

Hanover (Tegra)
Mallard (CG)
Matrix (Scangraphic)
Melior (Lino)
CG Melliza (CG)
Uranus (Alphatype)

Vermillion (III)

Helanna Script (Tegra)
Boston Script (Alphatype)
Embassy Script (Caslon)
Lucia Script (Lino)
Original Script (CG)
Typo Script (ATF)
Yorkshire Script (Alphatype)

Helios (CG)
Aekzidenz-Grotesk Buch (Berthold)
Aristocrat (Tegra)
Claro (Alphatype)
Europa Grotesk (Scangraphic)
Geneva (Autologic)
Hamilton (QMS)
Helvetica (Lino)
Megaron (Tegra)
Sonoran San Serif (IBM)
Spectra (III)
Swiss 721 (Bitstream)
CG Triumvirate (CG)

Helvetica (Lino)
Akzidenz-Grotesk Buch (Berthold)
Aristocrat (Tegra)
Claro (Alphatype)
Europa Grotesk (Scangraphic)
Geneva (Autologic)
Hamilton (QMS)
Helios (CG)
Megaron (Tegra)
Sonoran San Serif (IBM)
Spectra (III)
Swiss 721 (Bitstream)
CG Triumvirate (CG)

Highland (Tegra)
Calderon (Scangraphic)
Caledo (Alphatype)
Caledonia (Lino)
CG California (CG)
Gael (III)

Hobo (ATF)
Tramp (Autologic)

Horley Old Style (Monotype)
Horus Old Style (Autologic)
Dunkirk (Tegra)

Horus Old Style (Autologic)
Dunkirk (Tegra)
Horley Old Style (Monotype)

Hot Dog (Autologic)
Frankfurter (Letraset)

Humanist 531 (Bitstream)
Cintal (AM)
CG Symphony (CG)
Synchron (Scangraphic)
Syntax (Lino)
Synthesis (Autologic)

Humanist 777 (Bitstream)
Freeborn (Scangraphic)
CG Frontiera (CG)
Frutiger (Lino)
Provencale (Autologic)
Siegfried (AM)

Huxley Vertical (ATF)
Aldous Vertical (CG)

I

Ideal (Intertype)
Corinth (Autologic)
Ionic #5 (Lino)
Ionic #342 (Monotype)
News Text (Alphatype)
Regal (Intertype)

Imperial (Intertype)
Emperor (III)
Gazette (Lino)
New Bedford (Autologic)
News No. 4 (CG)

Incised 901 (Bitstream)
Alphavanti (Alphatype)
Antique Olive (Olive)
Berry Roman (III)
Oliva (Autologic)
Olive (AM)

Independence (Alphatype)
Americana (ATF)
American Classic (CG)
Colonial (Tegra)
Concord (III)
Freedom (Autologic)

Ionic #5 (Lino)
Corinth (Autologic)
Ideal (Intertype)
Ionic #342 (Monotype)
News Text (Alphatype)
Regal (Intertype)

Ionic #342 (Monotype)
Corinth (Autologic)
Ideal (Intertype)
Ionic #5 (Lino)
News Text (Alphatype)
Regal (Intertype)

Iridium (Lino)
Iron (Scangraphic)

Iron (Scangraphic)
Iridium (Lino)

Italian Script (Alphatype)
Venetian Script (CG)

J

Jan (Tegra)
Serpentine (Lino)

Janson
Dutch Oldstyle (CG)
Jason (Autologic)

Jason (Autologic)
Dutch Oldstyle (CG)
Janson

Jasper (CG)
Grayda (ATF)

K

Kabel (Lino)
Kobel (Alphatype)

Kaskade Script (Autologic)
Cascade Script (Lino)

Kaufman (Tegra)
Balloon (ATF)
Kaufman Script (ATF)
L.A. Script (Autologic)
Swing Bold (Monotype)
Tropez (CG)

Kaufman Script (ATF)
Balloon (ATF)
Kaufman (Tegra)
L.A. Script (Autologic)
Swing Bold (Monotype)
Tropez (CG)

Kaylin Script (Tegra)
French Script (CG)

Typo Upright (ATF)

Kennerley (Lan. Mono.)
Kenntonian (Harris)
Kensington (Autologic)
Kentuckian (Alphatype)

Kenntonian (Harris)
Kennerley (Lan. Mono.)
Kensington (Autologic)
Kentuckian (Alphatype)

Kensington (Autologic)
Kennerley (Lan. Mono.)
Kenntonian (Harris)
Kentuckian (Alphatype)

Kentuckian (Alphatype)
Kenntonian (Harris)
Kensington (Autologic)
Kentuckian (Alphatype)

Kobel (Alphatype)
Kabel (Lino)
Sans Serif (Lan. Mono.)

Koronna (Alphatype)
Aquarius (CG)
Cardinal (III)
Corona (Lino)
News No. 3 (CG)
News No. 5 (CG)
News No. 6 (CG)
Nimbus (Alphatype)
Royal (Intertype)

Kosmos (Xerox)
Alphavers (Alphatype)
Eterna (III)
CG Univers (CG)
Univers (D&P)
Versatile (Alphatype)

Kuenstler 480 (Bitstream)
Ascot (Autologic)
Mediaeval (AM)
Olympus (Alphatype)
Rennaissance (III)
Saul (Autologic)
CG Trump Mediaeval (CG)
Trump Mediaeval (Weber)

L

Latin 725 (Bitstream)
Equator (AM)

Latine (Autologic)
Maximal (CG)
Meridien (D&P)

Latine (Autologic)
Equator (Tegra)
Maximal (CG)
Meridian (III)
Meridien (D&P)

L.A. Script (Autologic)
Balloon (ATF)
Kaufman (Tegra)
Kaufman Script (ATF)
Swing Bold (Monotype)
Tropez (CG)

League Text (Alphatype)
Camelot (Tegra)
Esquire (Scangraphic)
Excel (Autologic)
Excelsior (Lino)
News No. 9 (CG)
News No. 14 (CG)

LeCochin (Berthold)
Cochin (Ludwig & Mayer)
Cochine (Autologic)
CG Collage (CG)
Gravure (Amsterdam)
Traverse (Tegra)

Liberty (CG)
Bernhard Cursive (ATF)
Bridal Script

Libra (Amsterdam)
Libretto (Alphatype)

Libretto (Alphatype)
Libra (Amsterdam)

Life (Simoncini)
Fredonia (Tegra)

Lisbon (CG)
Lydian (ATF)

Loren (III)
Torino (Nebiolo)

Lucia Script (Lino)
Boston Script (Alphatype)
Embassy Script (Caslon)
Formal Script (Ludlow)
Helanna Script (Tegra)
Original Script (CG)
Typo Script (ATF)

Yorkshire Script (Alphatype)

Lydian (ATF)
Lisbon (CG)

M

Magnum Gothic (CG)
Bank Gothic (ATF)
Bankers Gothic

Mahogany Script (CG)
Chapel Script (Photon)

Malibu (Autologic)
Compano (III)
CG Palacio (CG)
Paladium (CG)
Palatino (Lino)
Parlament (Scangraphic)
Patina (Alphatype)

Mallard (CG)
Hanover (Tegra)
Matrix (Scangraphic)
Melior (Lino)
CG Melliza (CG)
Uranus (Alphatype)
Vermillion (III)

Manchester Condensed (CG)
Century Nova (ATF)

Matrix (Scangraphic)
Hanover (Tegra)
CG Mallard (CG)
Melior (Lino)
CG Melliza (CG)
Metrion (ATF)
Uranus (Alphatype)
Vermillion (III)

Matt Antique (Itek)
Garth Graphic (CG)

Meandme (III)
Durante (Autologic)
Umbra (Ludlow)

Mediaeval (Tegra)
Ascot (Autologic)
Olympus (Alphatype)
Rennaissance (III)
Saul (Autologic)
CG Trump Mediaeval (CG)
Trump Mediaeval (Weber)

Megaron (Tegra)
Akzidenz-Grotesk Buch (Berthold)
Aristocrat (Tegra)
Claro (Alphatype)
Europa Grotesk (Scangraphic)
Geneva (Autologic)
Hamilton (QMS)
Helios (CG)
Helvetica (Lino)
Sonoran San Serif (IBM)
Spectra (III)
Swiss 721 (Bitstream)
CG Triumvirate (CG)

Melior (Lino)
Hanover (Tegra)
Mallard (CG)
Matrix (Scangraphic)
CG Melliza (CG)
Metrion (ATF)
Uranus (Alphatype)
Vermillion (III)

CG Melliza (CG)
Hanover (Tegra)
Mallard (CG)
Matrix (Scangraphic)
Melior (Lino)
Metrion (ATF)
Uranus (Alphatype)
Vermillion (III)

Memphis (Stempel)
Alexandria
Beton (Neufville)
Karnak (Ludlow)
CG Nashville (CG)
Pyramid (IBM)
Stymie (ATF)

Meridian (III)
Equator (Tegra)
Latine (Autologic)
Meridien (D&P)

Meridien (D&P)
Equator (Tegra)
Latine (Autologic)
Meridian (III)

Messenger (III)
Courier (IBM)
Courrier (Scangraphic)
Monaco (Apple)

Meteor (Autologic)

Gothic No. 2 (CG)
Gothic No. 3 (CG)
Metro (Lino)
Metromedium (III)

Metro (Lino)
Gothic No. 2 (CG)
Gothic No. 3 (CG)
Meteor (Autologic)
Metromedium (III)

Metromedium (III)
Gothic No. 2 (CG)
Gothic No. 3 (CG)
Meteor (Autologic)
Metro (Lino)

Microgramma (Nebiolo)
Aldostyle (Autologic)
Eurogothic (Alphatype)
Eurostile (Nebiolo)
Eurostyle (CG)
Gamma (III)
Microstyle (CG)

Microstyle (CG)
Aldostyle (Autologic)
Eurogothic (Alphatype)
Eurostile (Nebiolo)
Eurostyle (CG)
Gamma (III)
Microgramma (Nebiolo)

Minuet (Harris)
Continental Script (Autologic)
Piranesi Italic (ATF)

Mistral (Lino)
Aeolus (CG)

Modern (Tegra)
Craw Modern (ATF)

Monaco (Apple)
Courier (IBM)
Courrier (Scangraphic)
Messenger (III)

Monty (Alphatype)
Seraphim (Autologic)
Serifa (Lino)
Seriverse (Tegra)

Moore Computer
Computer (CG)

Murray (CG)
Murray Hill (ATF)

Murray Hill (ATF)
Murray (CG)

Musica (Alphatype)
Athena (Autologic)
October (Scangraphic)
CG Omega (CG)
Optima (Lino)
Optimist (Autologic)
Oracle (CG)
Roma (III)
Theme (IBM)

N

CG Nashville (CG)
Alexandria
Beton (Neufville)
Cairo (Intertype)
Karnak (Ludlow)
Memphis (Stempel)
Pyramid (IBM)
Stymie (ATF)

Neuzeit-Grotesk (Berthold)
Genneken (Tegra)
Grotesk-S (Scangraphic)

New Bedford (Autologic)
Emperor (III)
Gazette (Lino)
Imperial (Intertype)
News No. 4 (CG)

News Gothic (ATF)
Alpha Gothic (Alphatype)
Classified News (IBM)
CG Trade (CG)
Trade Gothic (Lino)

News No. 2 (CG)
Aurora (Lino)
News No. 12 (CG)

News No. 3 (CG)
Aquarius (CG)
Cardinal (III)
Corona (Lino)
Koronna (Alphatype)
News No. 5 (CG)
News No. 6 (CG)
Nimbus (Alphatype)
Royal (Intertype)

News No. 4 (CG)

Emperor (III)
Gazette (Lino)
Imperial (Intertype)
New Bedford (Autologic)

News No. 5 (CG)
Aquarius (CG)
Cardinal (III)
Corona (Lino)
Koronna (Alphatype)
News No. 3 (CG)
News No. 6 (CG)
Nimbus (Alphatype)
Royal (Intertype)

News 701 (Bitstream)
Corinth (Autologic)
Ideal (Intertype)
Ionic No. 5 (Lino)
Ionic No. 342 (Monotype)
News Text (Alphatype)
Regal (Intertype)

News 705 (Bitstream)
Aquarius (CG)
Cardinal (III)
Corona (Lino)
Koronna (Alphatype)
News No. 3 (CG)
News No. 5 (CG)
News No. 6 (CG)
Nimbus (Alphatype)
Royal (Intertype)

News No. 6 (CG)
Aquarius (CG)
Cardinal (III)
Corona (Lino)
Koronna (Alphatype)
News No. 3 (CG)
News No. 5 (CG)
Nimbus (Alphatype)
Royal (Intertype)

News No. 9 (CG)
Camelot (Tegra)
Esquire (Scangraphic)
Excel (Autologic)
Excelsior (Lino)
League Text (Alphatype)
News No. 14 (CG)

News No. 12 (CG)
Aurora (Lino)
News No. 2 (CG)

News No. 14 (CG)
Camelot (Tegra)
Esquire (Scangraphic)
Excel (Autologic)
Excelsior (Lino)
League Text (Alphatype)
News No. 9 (CG)

News Text (Alphatype)
Corinth (Autologic)
Ionic #5 (Lino)
Ionic #342 (Monotype)

New York (Apple)
Dutch 801 (Bitstream)
English (Alphatype)
English 49 (CG)
English Times (CG)
Press Roman (IBM)
CG Times (CG)
Sonoran Serif (IBM)
Times New Roman (Monotype)
Times Roman (Lino)
Varitimes (Tegra)

Nimbus (Alphatype)
Aquarius (CG)
Cardinal (III)
Corona (Lino)
Koronna (Alphatype)
News No. 3 (CG)
News No. 5 (CG)
News No 6 (CG)
Royal (Intertype)

Nordoff (Autologic)
Cheltenham (ATF)
Gloucester (Monotype)
Sorbonne (Berthold)
Winchester (Stephenson-Blake)

Noris Script (Lino)
Norris Script (Autologic)

Norris Script (Autologic)
Noris Script (Lino)

O

October (Scangraphic)
Athena (Autologic)
Musica (Alphatype)
CG Omega (CG)
Optima (Lino)

Optimist (Autologic)
Oracle (CG)
Roma (III)
Theme (IBM)

Old English #10
Yorkshire (CG)

Oliva (Autologic)
Alphavanti (Alphatype)
Antique Olive (Olive)
Berry Roman (III)
Olive (Tegra)

Olive (Tegra)
Alphavanti (Alphatype)
Antique Olive (Olive)
Berry Roman (III)
Oliva (Autologic)

Olympus (Alphatype)
Ascot (Autologic)
Mediaeval (Tegra)
Rennaissance (III)
Saul (Autologic)
CG Trump Mediaeval (CG)
Trump Mediaeval (Weber)

Olympian (Lino)
Olympus (Autologic)

Olympus (Autologic)
Olympian (Lino)

CG Omega (CG)
Athena (Autologic)
Musica (Alphatype)
October (Scangraphic)
Optima (Lino)
Optimist (Autologic)
Oracle (CG)
Roma (III)
Theme (IBM)

Operinia (Autologic)
Shelley (Lino)

Optima (Lino)
Athena (Autologic)
Musica (Alphatype)
October (Scangraphic)
CG Omega (CG)
Optimist (Autologic)
Oracle (CG)
Roma (III)
Theme (IBM)

Optimist (Autologic)
Athena (Autologic)
Musica (Alphatype)
October (Scangraphic)
CG Omega (CG)
Optima (Lino)
Oracle (CG)
Roma (III)
Theme (IBM)

Oracle (CG)
Athena (Autologic)
Musica (Alphatype)
October (Scangraphic)
CG Omega (CG)
Optima (Lino)
Optimist (Autologic)
Roma (III)
Theme (IBM)

Original Script (CG)
Boston Script (Alphatype)
Embassy Script (Caslon)
Florentine Script (Photon)
Helanna Script (Tegra)
Lucia Script (Lino)
Typo Script (ATF)
Yorkshire Script (Alphatype)

P

Pabst Extra Bold (Lino)
Cooper Black (ATF)

CG Palacio (CG)
Compano (III)
Malibu (Autologic)
Paladium (CG)
Palatino (Lino)
Parlament (Scangraphic)
Patina (Alphatype)

Paladium (CG)
Andover (Photon)
Compano (III)
Malibu (Autologic)
CG Palacio (CG)
Palatino (Lino)
Parlament (Scangraphic)
Patina (Alphatype)

Palatino (Lino)
Andover (Photon)
Compano (III)

Malibu (Autologic)
CG Palacio (CG)
Paladium (CG)
Parlament (Scangraphic)
Patina (Alphatype)

Palisade (Harris)
Bondoni Campanile (Ludlow)

Parlament (Scangraphic)
Andover (Photon)
Compano (III)
Malibu (Autologic)
CG Palacio (CG)
Paladium (CG)
Palatino (Lino)
Patina (Alphatype)

Patina (Alphatype)
Andover (Photon)
Compano (III)
Malibu (Autologic)
CG Palacio (CG)
Paladium (CG)
Palatino (Lino)
Parlament (Scangraphic)

Peignot (D&P)
Penyoe (CG)

Penman Script (Tegra)
Engravers Roundhand (Autologic)
Roundhand (Itek)
Roundhand No. 1 (Alphatype)
Signet Roundhand (CG)
Snell Roundhand (Lino)

Penyoe (CG)
Peignot (D&P)

Percepta (Alphatype)
Perpetua (Monotype)

Perpetua (Monotype)
Percepta (Alphatype)

Pharaoh (Autologic)
Egyptian Bold Condensed

Piranesi Italic (ATF)
Continental Script (Autologic)

Plantin
Atlantic (Alphatype)
CG Plantin (CG)

CG Plantin (CG)
Atlantic (Alphatype)

Plantin

Polka (Berthold)
Brush Roman (III)
Dom Casual (ATF)

Poppl-Pontifex (Berthold)
Brunswick (Tegra)
Power (Scangraphic)

Power (Scangraphic)
Brunswick (Tegra)
Poppl-Pontifex (Berthold)

Premier (Autologic)
Primer (Lino)
Rector (Alphatype)

Press Roman (IBM)
Dutch 801 (Bitstream)
English (Alphatype)
English 49 (CG)
English Times (CG)
New York (Apple)
Sonoran Serif (IBM)
CG Times (CG)
Times New Roman (Monotype)
Times Roman (Lino)
Varitimes (Tegra)

Primer (Lino)
Premier (Autologic)
Rector (Alphatype)

Provencale (Autologic)
born (Scangraphic)
CG Frontiera (CG)
Frutiger (Lino)
Siegfried (Tegra)

Pyramid (IBM)
Alexandria
Cairo (Intertype)
Karnak (Ludlow)
Memphis (Stempel)
CG Nashville (CG)
Stymie (ATF)

Q

Quill (CG)
Quill Script (Tegra)
Quillscript (Itek)
Thompson Quill Script (ATF)

Quillscript (Itek)

Quill (CG)
Quill Script (Tegra)
Thompson Quill Script (ATF)

Quill Script (Tegra)
Quill (CG)
Quillscript (Itek)
Thompson Quill Script (ATF)

R

Radiant (Ludlow)
Chatsworth (Autologic)

Rector (Alphatype)
Premier (Autologic)
Primer (Lino)

Regal (Intertype)
Corinth (Autologic)
Ideal (Intertype)
Ionic #5 (Lino)
Ionic #342 (Monotype)
News Text (Alphatype)

Rennaissance (III)
Ascot (Autologic)
Mediaeval (Tegra)
Olympus (Alphatype)
Saul (Autologic)
CG Trump Mediaeval (CG)
Trump Mediaeval (Weber)

Rhea (Tegra)
Derek Italic (CG)
Doric Black (Lino)

Riga (Autologic)
Auriga (Lino)

Riveria (Photon)
Ronde Text

Roma (III)
Athena (Autologic)
Musica (Alphatype)
October (Scangraphic)
CG Omega (CG)
Optima (Lino)
Optimist (Autologic)
Oracle (CG)
Theme (IBM)

Roman Stylus (CG)
Antique Open (Lino)
Typo Roman Open (ATF)

Rotation (Lino)
Rotieren (Autologic)

Rotieren (Autologic)
Rotation (Lino)

Roundhand (Itek)
Engravers Roundhand (Autologic)
Penman Script (Tegra)
Roundhand No. 1 (Alphatype)
Signet Roundhand (CG)
Snell Roundhand (Lino)

Roundhand No. 1 (Alphatype)
Engravers Roundhand (Autologic)
Penman Script (Tegra)
Roundhand (Itek)
Signet Roundhand (CG)
Snell Roundhand (Lino)

Royal (Intertype)
Aquarius (CG) `
Cardinal (III)
Corona (Lino)
Koronna (Alphatype)
News No. 3 (CG)
News No. 5 (CG)
News No. 6 (CG)
Nimbus (Alphatype)

Ruhr (III)
Aachen (Letraset)
Charlemagne (Tegra)

S

Sabon
Berner (Tegra)
September (Scangraphic)
Sybil (Autologic)

Saul (Autologic)
Ascot (Autologic)
Continental (Harris)
Mediaeval (Tegra)
Olympus (Alphatype)
Rennaissance (III)
CG Trump Mediaeval (CG)
Trump Mediaeval (Weber)

Schoolbook (Tegra)
Century Medium (IBM)
Century Schoolbook (ATF)
Century Text (Alphatype)
Century Textbook (CG)

Selectra (Autologic)
Avanta (III)
Elante (CG)
Electra (Lino)

September (Scangraphic)
Berner (Tegra)
Sabon
Sybil (Autologic)

Seraphim (Autologic)
Monty (Alphatype)
Serifa (Lino)
Seriverse (Tegra)

Serifa (Lino)
Monty (Alphatype)
Seraphim (Autologic)
Seriverse (Tegra)

Seriverse (Tegra)
Monty (Alphatype)
Serifa (Lino)
Seraphim (Autologic)

Serpentine (Lino)
Jan (Tegra)

Shelley (Lino)
Operinia (Autologic)

Siegfried (Tegra)
Freeborn (Scangraphic)
CG Frontiera (CG)
Frutiger (Lino)
Provencale (Autologic)

Signet Roundhand (CG)
Engravers Roundhand (Autologic)
Penman Script (Tegra)
Roundhand (Itek)
Roundhand No. 1 (Alphatype)
Snell Roundhand (Lino)

Snell Roundhand (Lino)
Engravers Roundhand (Autologic)
Penman Script (Tegra)
Roundhand (Itek)
Roundhand No. 1 (Alphatype)
Signet Roundhand (CG)

Sonoran Sans Serif (IBM)
Akzidenz-Grotesk Buch (Berthold)
Aristocrat (Tegra)
Claro (Alphatype)
Europa Grotesk (Scangraphic)
Hamilton (QMS)

Helios (CG)
Helvetica (Lino)
Geneva (Autologic)
Megaron (Tegra)
Spectra (III)
Swiss 721 (Bitstream)
CG Triumvirate (CG)

Sonoran Serif (IBM)
Dutch 801 (Bitstream)
English (Alphatype)
English 49 (CG)
English Times (CG)
New York (Apple)
Press Roman (IBM)
CG Times (CG)
Times New Roman (Monotype)
Times Roman (Lino)
Varitimes (Tegra)

Sorbonne (Berthold)
Cheltenham (ATF)
Gloucester (Monotype)
Nordoff (Autologic)
Winchester (Stephenson-Blake)

Sparta (Autologic)
Alphatura (Alphatype)
Futura (Bauer)
Future (Alphatype)
Spartan (Lino)
Technica (III)
Twentieth Century (Monotype)

Spartan (Lino)
Alphatura (Alphatype)
Futura (Bauer)
Future (Alphatype)
Sparta (Autologic)
Technica (III)
Twentieth Century (Monotype)

Spartan (Monotype)
Copperplate
Copperplate Gothic (ATF)

Spectra (III)
Akzidenz-Grotesk Buch (Berthold)
Aristocrat (Tegra)
Claro (Alphatype)
Europa Grotesk (Scangraphic)
Hamilton (QMS)
Helios (CG)
Helvetica (Lino)
Geneva (Autologic)

Megaron (Tegra)
Sonoran Sans Serif (IBM)
Swiss 721 (Bitstream)
CG Triumvirate (CG)

Square 721 (Bitstream)
Aldostyle (Autologic)
Eurogothic (Alphatype)
Eurostile (Nebiolo)
Eurostyle (CG)
Gamma (III)
Microgramma (Nebiolo)
Microstyle (CG)

Standard (Berthold)
Ad Grotesk (Scangraphic)

Stuyvesant (CG)
Wintergreen (Tegra)

Stymie (ATF)
Alexandria
Cairo (Intertype)
Memphis (Stempel)
CG Nashville (CG)
Pyramid (IBM)

Swing Bold (Monotype)
Balloon (ATF)
Kaufman (Tegra)
Kaufman Script (ATF)
L.A. Script (Autologic)
Tropez (CG)

Swiss 721 (Bitstream)
Akzidenz-Grotesk Buch (Berthold)
Aristocrat (Tegra)
Claro (Alphatype)
Europa Grotesk (Scangraphic)
Hamilton (QMS)
Helios (CG)
Helvetica (Lino)
Geneva (Autologic)
Megaron (Tegra)
Sonoran San Serif (IBM)
Spectra (III)
CG Triumvirate (CG)

Sybil (Autologic)
Berner (Tegra)
Sabon September (Scangraphic)

CG Symphony (CG)
Cintal (Tegra)
Synchron (Scangraphic)
Syntax (Lino)

Synthesis (Autologic)

Synchron (Scangraphic)
Cintal (Tegra)
CG Symphony (CG)
Syntax (Lino)
Synthesis (Autologic)

Syntax (Lino)
Cintal (Tegra)
CG Symphony (CG)
Synchron (Scangraphic)
Synthesis (Autologic)

Synthesis (Autologic)
Cintal (Tegra)
CG Symphony (CG)
Synchron (Scangraphic)
Syntax (Lino)

T

Technica (III)
Alphatura (Alphatype)
Futura (Bauer)
Future (Alphatype)
Sparta (Autologic)
Spartan (Lino)
Twentieth Century (Monotype)

Techno (Photon)
Alphatura (Alphatype)
Futura (Bauer)
Future (Alphatype)
Sparta (Autologic)
Spartan (Lino)
Technica (III)
Twentieth Century (Monotype)

Theme (IBM)
Athena (Autologic)
Chelmsford (Photon)
Musica (Alphatype)
October (Scangraphic)
CG Omega (CG)
Optima (Lino)
Optimist (Autologic)
Oracle (CG)
Roma (III)

Thompson Quill Script (ATF)
Quill (CG)
Quillscript (Itek)
Quill Script (Tegra)

CG Times (CG)
Dutch 801 (Bitstream)
English (Alphatype)
English 49 (CG)
English Times (CG)
New York (Apple)
Press Roman (IBM)
Sonoran Serif (IBM)
Times Roman (Lino)
Times New Roman (Monotype)
Varitimes (Tegra)

Times New Roman (Monotype)
Dutch 801 (Bitstream)
English (Alphatype)
English 49 (CG)
English Times (CG)
New York (Apple)
Press Roman (IBM)
Sonoran Serif (IBM)
CG Times (CG)
Times Roman
Varitimes (Tegra)

Times Roman (Lino)
Dutch 801 (Bitstream)
English (Alphatype)
English 49 (CG)
English Times (CG)
New York (Apple)
Press Roman (IBM)
Sonoran Serif (IBM)
CG Times (CG)
Times New Roman (Monotype)
Varitimes (Tegra)

Torino (Nebiolo)
Loren (III)

Tower (ATF)
City (Berthold)
Town (Autologic)

Town (Autologic)
City (Berthold)
Tower (ATF)

CG Trade (CG)
Alpha Gothic (Alphatype)
Classified News (IBM)
News Gothic (ATF)
Trade Gothic (Lino)

Trade Gothic (Lino)
Alpha Gothic (Alphatype)

Classified News (IBM)
News Gothic (ATF)
CG Trade (CG)

Trajanus (Stempel)
Akiba (Autologic)
Viceroy (Tegra)

Tramp (Autologic)
Hobo (ATF)

Transitional 511 (Bitstream)
Caledo (Alphatype)
Calderon (Scangraphic)
Caledonia (Lino)
CG California (CG)
Gael (III)
Highland (AM)

Transitional 521 (Bitstream)
Avante (III)
Elante (CG)
Electra (Lino)
Selectra (Autologic)

Transitional 551 (Bitstream)
Fairfield (Lino)
Fairefax (Autologic)
Fairmont (Alphatype)

Transport (Tegra)
Chinchilla (Scangraphic)
Concert (Alphatype)
Concorde (Berthold)

Traverse (Tegra)
Cochin (Ludwig & Mayer)
Cochine (Autologic)
CG Collage (CG)
LeCochin (Berthold)

CG Triumvirate (CG)
Akzidenz-Grotesk Buch (Berthold)
Aristocrat (Tegra)
Claro (Alphatype)
Europa Grotesk (Scangraphic)
Hamilton (QMS)
Helios (CG)
Helvetica (Lino)
Geneva (Autologic)
Megaron (Tegra)
Newton (Photon)
Sonoran San Serif (IBM)
Spectra (III)
Swiss 721 (Bitstream)

Tropez (CG)
Balloon (ATF)
Kaufman (Tegra)
Kaufman Script (ATF)
L.A. Script (Autologic)
Swing Bold (Monotype)

CG Trump Mediaeval (CG)
Ascot (Autologic)
Mediaeval (Tegra)
Olympus (Alphatype)
Rennaissance (III)
Saul (Autologic)
Trump Mediaeval (Weber)

Trump Mediaeval (Weber)
Ascot (Autologic)
Mediaeval (Tegra)
Olympus (Alphatype)
Rennaissance (III)
Saul (Autologic)
CG Trump Mediaeval (CG)

Twentieth Century (Monotype)
Alphatura (Alphatype)
Futura (Bauer)
Future (Alphatype)
Sparta (Autologic)
Spartan (Lino)
Technica (III)

Typo Roman Open (ATF)
Antique Open (Lino)
Roman Stylus (CG)

Typo Roman (ATF)
Antique Solid (Lino)

Typo Script
Boston Script (Alphatype)
Formal Script (Ludlow)
Helanna Script (Tegra)
Lucia Script (Lino)
Original Script (CG)
Yorkshire Script (Alphatype)

Typo Upright (ATF)
French Script (CG)
Kaylin Script (Tegra)

U

Umbra (Berthold)
Durante (Autologic)
Meandme (III)

CG Univers (CG)
Alphavers (Alphatype)
Eterna (III)
Kosmos (Xerox)
Univers (D&P)
Versatile (Alphatype)

Univers (D&P)
Alphavers (Alphatype)
Eterna (III)
Kosmos (Xerox)
CG Univers (CG)
Versatile (Alphatype)

University Roman (Letraset)
Ace (Itek)

Uranus (Alphatype)
Hanover (Tegra)
Mallard (CG)
Matrix (Scangraphic)
Melior (Lino)
CG Melliza (CG)
Metrion (ATF)
Vermillion (III)

V

Varitimes (Tegra)
Dutch 801 (Bitstream)
English (Alphatype)
English 49 (CG)
English Times (CG)
New York (Apple)
Press Roman (IBM)
CG Times (CG)
Sonoran Serif (IBM)
Times New Roman (Monotype)
Times Roman (Lino)

Vascones Text (Autologic)
Basque (Lino)

Venetian Script (CG)
Italian Script (Alphatype)

Versatile (Alphatype)
Alphavers (Alphatype)
Eterna (III)
Kosmos (Xerox)
CG Univers (CG)
Univers (D&P)

Vermillion (III)
Ballardvale (Photon)

Hanover (Tegra)
Mallard (CG)
Matrix (Scangraphic)
Melior (Lino)
CG Melliza (CG)
Uranus (Alphatype)

Viceroy (Tegra)
Akiba (Autologic)
Trajanus (Stempel)

W

Weiss (Bauer)
Edelweiss (Alphatype)

Whedon's Gothic Outline (ATF)
Gothic Outline (Tegra)
Gothic Outline Condensed (CG)

Winchester (Stephenson-Blake)
Cheltenham (ATF)
Gloucester (Monotype)
Nordoff (Autologic)
Sorbonne (Berthold)

Windsor (Stephenson-Blake)
Winslow (Alphatype)
Windsor (Stephenson-Blake)

Wintergreen (Tegra)

Stuyvesant (CG)

Woop De Doo Bold (Tegra)
Gold Nugget (CG)
Gold Rush (ATF)

Y

Yorkshire (CG)
Old English #10

Yorkshire Script (Alphatype)
Boston Script (Alphatype)
Formal Script (Ludlow)
Helanna Script (Tegra)
Lucia Script (Lino)
Original Script (CG)
Type Script (ATF)

Z

Zapf Calligraphic 801 (Bitstream)
Palatino (Lino)
Compano (III)
Malibu (Autologic)
CG Palacio (CG)
Paladium (CG)
Parlament (Scangraphic)
Patina (Alphatype)

Zapf Elliptical 711 (Bitstream)
Hanover (AM)
Mallard (CG)
Matrix (Scangraphic)
Melior (Lino)
CG Melliza (CG)
Matrion (ATF)
Uranus (Alphatype)
Vermillion (III)

Zapf Humanist 601 (Bitstream)
Athena (Autologic)
Chelmsford (Photon)
Musica (Alphatype)
October (Scangraphic)
CG Omega (CG)
Optima (Lino)
Optimist (Autologic)
Oracle (CG)
Roma (III)
Theme (IBM)

Zurich (Bitstream)
Alphavers (Alphatype)
Eterna (III)
Kosmos (Xerox)
CG Univers (CG)
Univers (D&P)
Versatile (Alphatype)

BIBLIOGRAPHY

Carter, Sebastian. *Twentieth-Century Type Designers*. New York: Taplinger, 1987.

Gray, Nicolete. *A History of Lettering*. Oxford: Phaidon, 1986.

Haley, Allan. *Phototypography: A Guide to In-House Typesetting and Design*. New York: Scribner's, 1980.

Hlasta, Stanley C. *Printing Types and How to Use Them*. Pittsburgh: Carnegie Press, 1950.

Jaspert, W. Pincus, W. Turner Berry, and A. F. Johnson. *Encyclopedia of Typefaces*. Poole: Blandford Press, 1953.

Lawson, A., and A. Provan. *One Hundred Type Histories*. 2 vols. Arlington, Va.: National Composition Association, 1983.

Lieberman, J. Benn. *Type and Typefaces*. New Rochelle, N.Y.: Myriade Press, 1978.

McGrew, Mac. *American Metal Typefaces of the Twentieth Century*. New Rochelle, N.Y.: Myriade Press, 1986.

Meriman, Frank. *ATA Type Comparison Book*. New York: Advertising Typographers of America, 1965.

Meynell, Francis, and Herbert Simcon. *Fleuron Anthology*. Toronto: University of Toronto Press, Ernest Benn, 1973.

Perfect, Christopher, and Gordon Rookledge. *Rookledge's International Typefinder*. New York: Frederic C. Biel, 1983.

Tracy, Walter. *Letters of Credit: A View of Type Design*. Boston: David R. Godine, 1986.

Updike, Daniel Berkeley. *Printing Types: Their History, Forms, and Use—A Study in Survivals*. Cambridge, Mass.: Harvard University Press, 1922.

Wallis, L. W. *Type Design Developments, 1970 to 1985*. Arlington, Va.: National Composition Association, 1985.

Weinberger, Norman S. *Encyclopedia of Comparative Letterforms for Artists and Designers*. New York: Art Direction Book Company, 1971.

Index

INDEX